T0386539

EDEN'S KEEPERS

Gardens designed by Humphrey Waterfield

Hill Pasture, Broxted, Essex
Ashgrove Cottage, Broxted, Essex
Greys Court, National Trust, Henley, Oxfordshire
Abbots Ripton Hall, Cambridgeshire
Le Clos du Peyronnet, Menton, France
The Chase, Ugley, Essex

EDEN'S KEEPERS

The Lives and Gardens of
Humphrey Waterfield & Nancy Tennant

Sarah Barclay

"Some natural tears they dropped, but wiped them soon;
The world was all before them, where to choose their place of rest,
and Providence their guide: They hand in hand with wand'ring
steps and slow, through Eden took their solitary way."
Paradise Lost

I am your wife, if you will marry me:
If not, I'll die your maid: to be your fellow
You may deny me, but I'll be your servant,
Whether you will or no.
(Miranda, Act 3 Scene 1) *The Tempest*

CLEARVIEW BOOKS

First published in the UK in 2022 by Clearview Books
99 Priory Park Road, London NW6 7UX
www.clearviewbooks.com

Text © Sarah Barclay
Compilation © Clearview Books
© Photograph No 2 Saffron Walden Society
© Photograph No 3 Nell Carey
© Photograph No 4 &6 Tiddy Maitland-Titterton, courtesy of Nell Carey
© Photograph No 5,9,10 Laura Russell
©Photograph No 7&8 Tanera Averdeick
© Photograph No 11,12,13,14,15,16,17,18,19,20,24,25,26,29,30,33,34,35,36,37,42,44,45,46,47,
52,55,56,57,67 William Waterfield courtesy of 06 Département des Alpes-Maritimes
© Photograph No 21 Reproduced by permission of the Provost and Fellows of Eton College
© Photograph No 22,27,28,32,58,62 Giles Waterfield Archive, Paul Mellon Centre London
© Photograph No 23,53,54 National Federation of Women's Institute
© Photograph No 38,41,48,49,50,51 Alamy
© Photograph No 39,40,43 Britain Yearly Meeting
© Photograph No 59,61,63,64,65,66 Future Content Hub
© Photograph No 60 Amateur Gardening London

Extracts from Nancy Tennant's letters and memoirs are reproduced by kind
permission of the trustees of the estate of A.D. Tennant. All rights reserved.

ISBN 978-1908337-634

Editor: Catharine Snow
Production: Rosanna Dickinson
Picture Research: Marie Henckel
Design and typeset: Palimpsest Book Production Ltd, Falkirk, Stirlingshire
Printed and bound in Great Britain by Clays Ltd, Elcograf S.p.A

A CIP record of this book is available from the British Library.

For Dingus, Alexander and Eliza

Contents

Dramatis Personae

FAMILY OF NANCY TENNANT

Parents:	William Tennant and Agnes Gairdner
Brothers:	Ernest Tennant
	'Bunny' Charles Alan Tennant
Sister:	Margaret Mercer, afterwards Margaret Birley
Niece:	Ariel Mercer
Other	Sir Charles Tennant
	Christopher Tennant (2nd Baron Glenconner)
	Colin Tennant (3rd Baron Glenconner)
	Margot Asquith
	Pamela Wyndham
	Stephen Tennant

FAMILY OF HUMPHREY WATERFIELD

Parents:	Barbara Gardner and Frederick 'Derick' Waterfield
Sister:	Sylvie Waterfield (deceased)
Brother:	Anthony 'Tony' Waterfield
Other	John Pritt Gardner
	Sarah Bertha Pearson
	Meta Gardner
	Duncan and Violet Gardner

FRIENDS AMBULANCE UNIT

Peter Townsend
Stephen Verney
Frederick 'Freddy' Temple
Hamilton 'Hammy' Mills
Raymond 'Nik' Alderson

ART WORLD

Clive Bell
Vanessa Bell
Duncan Grant
Albert Rutherston

NAZI GERMANY

Joachim von Ribbentrop
Adolf Hitler
Ernst 'Putzi' Hanfstaengl

ORGANISATIONS

National Federation of Women's Institutes
Bach Choir
The National Trust
Friends Ambulance Unit
Anglo-German Fellowship

LOCATIONS

England, Scotland, France, Italy, Greece, Turkey, Syria, Lebanon,
Egypt, Libya, Tunisia

Eden's Keepers

Humphrey Waterfield and Nancy Tennant were life-long partners. Together they created the most beautiful small garden in England.

But there was more to Hill Pasture than met the eye. Although hailed as a living work of art and an outstanding garden design, it was more than simply an exquisite horticultural triumph. Hill Pasture was a camouflage, providing joy and consolation for the traumas and frustrated passions of youth.

This challenging love story of paradise lost, found and lost again, is set against the backdrop of the 20th century, the traumas of two world wars, polarised British politics, the changing position of women in society, the transformative power of the natural world, and the best of human love.

SARAH BARCLAY

Prologue

Humphrey Waterfield and Nancy Tennant gazed at the three-acre meadow, which had been the village dump. It seemed an unloved, forgotten, scrappy sort of place, heavy with the aroma of sun-warmed stinging nettles and the flat, green scent of couch grass. The hum of a thousand busy insects filled the air. To the west stretched a lovely valley of interlocking fields and when they turned east, a copse of ash and willow met their gaze. There was shelter as well as a view. Tender plants could thrive here. The two friends regarded the sloping field once more and decided it would do very well. The position was perfect.

~

This peaceful patch of England was to become the centre of their world, their romantic earthly paradise, a publicly acclaimed work of art and a consolation for the loss and trauma of their pasts. It would also provide a smokescreen for their deepest feelings, even for each other. And, one day, the smoke would begin to clear and the truth of who, and how they really loved would be plain to see. It wasn't what it appeared to be, at all.

CHAPTER ONE

The Unloved Son

1907

'He and his mother had never discussed the feelings between them: in the English manner both thought it better not to discuss personal problems openly. Instead, one hoped such emotions would soon be forgotten.'
Giles Waterfield The Long Afternoon

It couldn't be done. Surrendering to unfettered maternal love was beyond contemplation for Barbara Waterfield. As she stood alone on the ship's deck and watched the shrouded bundle that had been her first-born slip under the surface of the Red Sea, she shut down. Grief-stricken and traumatised by the loss of baby Sylvia, by the time her second child entered the world two years later, her heart had already hardened. Underneath she may have been bursting with pride at her vigorous, healthy boy but any outward displays of affection would, from then on, be subject to the barriers of emotional self-preservation.

Before Sylvia's death, motherhood had held so much promise. Now it no longer felt safe. The quickening flicker of anxiety collapsing into helpless dread that she had felt so acutely on that boat would define her adult life. Germs, contagion and journeys from one continent to another would be her greatest fear, and at the very end, her undoing. Her second born, Humphrey, would pay the price.

The boat on the Red Sea was a long way from her beginnings. Born on the 10th December 1878 in Rugeley, Staffordshire, she was a materially fortunate, only child. Her home was Hagley Hall, a sprawling country house, which had been bought by her father, John Pritt Gardner, a successful lawyer. It was a romantic looking confection of varied architectural styles, not on the scale of a grand stately home, but nevertheless a substantial, solid building of generous proportions built over three centuries. The landscaped park that surrounded it included a series of lakes, a folly and an ornamental bridge.

Beautiful and comfortable her surroundings may have been, but Barbara's emotional foundations were less robust. John Gardner was deserted by Barbara's mother when she was young. The young Bertha Sarah Pearson had eloped with the local doctor and, according to the family, was never heard from again. They were divorced in 1886. There is no mention of her name in Barbara's engagement announcement to Humphrey's father many years later. Fortunately, the absence of her mother was tempered by the presence of her 'clever and attractive' spinster aunt, Meta, John Gardner's sister, who moved to Hagley following Bertha's desertion, to take on the role of châtelaine. Over ten years younger than her brother, according to Duncan Gardner, her nephew, *'a good-looking brunette with a shapely figure, about five foot six inches tall, turning a trifle solid in middle age. Without laying any claim to intellect, she had fully average wits and all the 'right' upper-middle class manners and mores; played tennis croquet and billiards with skill and elegance, and was amiable with children, who liked her.'* She may have been described by Humphrey as 'a good aunt' but, in the end, she was not Barbara's mother. Maternal love was absent.

Following the conventions of the day, Barbara would expect to have been married by her 18th birthday but was still a spinster, on the shelf at 25; surprising as her status as an only child meant she was an heiress. Anxieties about whether it was because her mother was a bolter, with all the attending scandal, did sometimes occur to Barbara. Had it put off all the available, young men? It was true that, because of the English laws of primogeniture which meant that eldest sons inherited all the family assets (if there were any), for the second, third and subsequent sons this meant earning a living. To achieve this they often went to the colonies, India and Kenya being particular favourites. The choice there was either to make their fortune or settle down to a reliable job with a regular income in a comfortable, colonial life, and only then were they able to take a wife. In 'The Fishing Fleet', Anne de Courcy charts the flow of hopeful young women to India in the 19th and 20th centuries in search of a husband.

Luckily Barbara did not have to join the fishing fleet. According to Giles Waterfield, her grandson, she was 'unearthed' in England by Derick Waterfield on a reverse wife-hunting visit from India. She was older than the conventional bride but the security of her financial prospects overrode any concerns in that quarter. She accepted Derick's proposal.

Derick's father, Sir Henry Waterfield was an eminent figure in the Indian Empire and by the time he retired, highly decorated. As Private Secretary to successive Indian Heads of State it was no surprise that his son followed in his footsteps and worked in the Indian Civil Service. Barbara and Derick were quickly engaged and on 27th October, 1905 the young couple were married in St Thomas's Cathedral, Bombay, India, the grandest of colonial churches in the city. Within a year Barbara was pregnant and left the heat of India for the clemency and familiar surroundings of Hagley Hall. In the spring of 1907, Sylvia Waterfield was born. Once the baby was a few months old, it was time to return and Barbara booked their passage ready to begin her life as a colonial wife and mother. She was to travel by steamship: a comfortable and appealing prospect. She and her tiny daughter would journey together through Europe, passing down the west coast of France, Spain and Portugal, along the North African coastline, down through the Suez Canal to India.

In the two years since Barbara had sailed over to England, disease on board was still rife. In spite of rigorous medical inspections prior to setting sail and daily ones throughout the journey, serious illness and even death were not uncommon. Once more in *The Fishing Fleet*, Anne de Courcy describes the death of an infant 'a few months old' witnessed by Florence Evans on SS Nubia at the same time Barbara would have been travelling to India. On that boat 'scarlatina' (scarlet fever today) had infected some of the children. One died and, as was customary, buried at sea. However, on Barbara's ship, whether due to dehydration, or some other cause, little Sylvia Waterfield faded from life as the boat powered remorselessly through the Red Sea.

By the time Barbara arrived in India, the terminal dangers of the east made her determined to remove her husband from Indian colonial life. She was convinced he had tuberculosis or a weak constitution, so Derick cut short a promising career and the couple retreated to England and to Hagley. Barbara may have shared the misery of Sylvia's death with her aunt Meta, and perhaps she was even lovingly comforted by her, but it is unlikely she would have had much warmth or consolation from her father. In a memoir written by Duncan Gardner, a cousin, he remembered his uncle John with mixed feelings. *'He seemed to take little or no interest in children, though he had one of his own, Barbara, later Waterfield. The thickness of his emotional skin is illustrated by his remark to a young mother who was distraught by the death of her first baby, 'Pooh, young woman, you can easily get another.'* Whether Duncan Gardner was directly describing Barbara's father's reaction to the death of his first grandchild or someone else is unclear, but the lack of compassion, whoever it was directed at was marked.

Two years later, on 7th August 1908 Barbara gave birth to a boy,

Humphrey. The following year, another son, Tony, arrived. By simply living longer than baby Sylvia, Humphrey bolstered his mother's confidence to believe her children would survive, but the real beneficiary of that confidence was Tony who enjoyed much more maternal affection than his elder brother. At least that is how Humphrey perceived it.

Derick Waterfield may have been more emotionally stable than his wife but, by the time their first and second sons had arrived, had developed a weak chest, fulfilling his wife's hoped-for prophecy. There was no question of returning to India: Barbara took the opportunity to announce he would have been a medical liability in the searing heat, dust and monsoon humidity. Yet Staffordshire and Hagley, beautiful as they were, were too cold and damp. The Waterfields must go south. A move to the warmer climes of Cornwall seemed at first to be the solution. The couple decided to try living in Marazion, a pretty holiday town opposite St Michael's Mount. However, by 1912, Derick's health had not improved. The Mediterranean beckoned.

The world, or at least the world that Barbara was prepared to live in, was now their oyster; the Waterfields had come into a fortune. Barbara's father had died the year before and as the heiress to the sizeable sum her father had left her (almost £10 million in today's money), she was now rich. Hagley remained in the family, with Meta at the helm. The couple took off for the South of France with their boys. They rented at first, but soon found themselves an imposing villa to buy in the small resort of Menton, overlooking the Mediterranean Sea. It wasn't an onerous move for Derick Waterfield. Familiar with living in India, far from the green fields of England, a life in France was positively on the doorstep. A railway line had been built running along the Cote D'Azur and, since 1869, Menton's own station served the town; there was even a stop yards from the entrance to the villa.

Menton in the nineteenth and early twentieth century itself was a destination for languid, often consumptive, upper class British and

European aristocracy. The French historian Paul Gonnet was to remark, '*doctors send to our shores a colony of pale and listless English women and listless sons of nobility near death.*' A stone's throw from the Italian border, the area had its own microclimate, considered temperate and restorative compared to the extreme weather of the other towns along the coast. Menton was never racy like Antibes or Cannes where the F Scott Fitzgerald 'Riviera Set' partied so hard and self destructively. Its society at the turn of the century was reassuringly familiar to British expatriates. There was a tennis club which Derick would eventually preside over, a croquet society and an amateur dramatics troupe. The town operated socially like a far-flung outpost of the Empire, with absolutely no requirement to mix with the local residents.

Today, Menton is still as sophisticated and well maintained as it was in the early 1900's. Superficially it is a typical South of France Riviera town, complete with the sharp buzz of mopeds and the rumble of traffic up and down a beach-lined, coastal road but it also has an other-worldly quality. Steep, fairy-tale like limestone hills rise sharply behind the town, partly obscuring the wild *garrigue* growing around them. The view out to sea is a perfect steady azure. Ignoring the blocks of flats and post-1950's architecture, it isn't difficult to imagine the place the Waterfields made their home. Menton may be located near the urban sprawl of Monte Carlo but the simple fishing village of terracotta and soft, cinnamon-coloured buildings it once was, still prevails. To the young married couple, Menton and the villa they decided to buy, Le Clos du Peyronnet, felt like paradise.

In later years, Humphrey had a conflicted relationship with his French childhood home. He adored the gardens, which he viewed as a demi-Eden with lush tropical foliage full of the wonders of nature: '*This hot explosive world of actuality, where snakes glided mauve over hissing stones, of green tree frogs and fireflies burning up the nights of May . . . and the beauty of the Passion Flower, the incandescent trumpets of the Morning Glories consuming in one scorched flush of red and purple the brilliance of the sunbaked earth'* he wrote, years later, still enthralled. The house itself, however, was for him a place of stifling inertia and ineffectual Edwardian entitlement. Over the next few years, a steady pattern was to emerge. The family would live in Menton for the winter but return 'home' to England and Hagley, by then Humphrey's other 'paradise', in the summer. This regular migration, from an early age, was to influence Humphrey's idea of himself as transient and rootless, not entirely belonging anywhere in particular.

Travelling back to England to escape the heat of a Riviera summer was no hardship and he loved staying with his beloved Great Aunt Meta, who was still chatelaine at Hagley. In later life he would wallow in sentimental memories over these Hagley summers, reflecting on the weeks spent as a young boy, exploring the natural idyll that surrounded him, its landscapes and gardens, rejoicing in the comparatively mild English sunshine. Hagley was inextricably bound up with his sense of beauty, nature and his place in the world. *'Were I to conceive of Heaven, it would be no otherwise than Hagley, a Hagley laid up in Heaven, as the Platonic image of itself. For Hagley has drawn to itself all the vision of beauty of the world, its hill is the seat of the muses, its wind the wild west wind that bears in on it all the fragmentary beauty of the world, all the tattered dreams of poets and painters and musicians, all the humility and patience of all noble and chivalrous souls'* he wrote in 1940.

The convenient train and ferry from France to England allowed for a reasonably straightforward journey for the young Waterfield boys to embark on an English education, as was traditional for all male Waterfields. For Humphrey, boarding school meant separation from, and yearning for, absent pleasures, whether the soothing clemency and beauty of Hagley or the warmth and exotic balm of Menton. *'The long years in the South of France meant to us children interminable exile, at the back of our dreams, waking or sleeping was Hagley, a Hagley we were incapable of visualising which nevertheless we felt to be our true home. The blue Mediterranean, the white shuttered houses, had a smaller part in our affections. We sighed for a world of varnished grass, slow moving water, beech trees. We longed for rain and grey skies and snow. At last armistice came.'*

It was time to go to school in England. As Humphrey wrote in his autobiographical essay on childhood, 'The Trees', his rude awakening to a prep school education, at the end of the First World War, was a miserable experience.

CHAPTER TWO

Charmed Arrivistes

1897

There's a large portrait in a Hampshire farmhouse of a girl. Painted by her brother at the turn of the 20th century, it hangs cosily in the low ceilinged, beamed sitting-room of her great niece. The loose brushwork reveals an informality and warmth in the hand of the artist. A plain, long-faced, shy looking child stares into the distance from under a large straw hat. Her simple blue dress is fastened loosely at the waist with a boyish brown leather belt.

She is standing in a garden, but not a garden of flowers and bright blue sky. The landscape around her is brooding and dark, with trees, heavy in late summer leaf, framing her. A gloomy redbrick building rises up behind her but does not overwhelm – rather, she seems able to be define her own space. Her surroundings are giving no concession to her youth, femininity or even fragility. In fact, she doesn't appear to be fragile at all. Was this a clever insight from Ernest, her sibling, ten years her senior, as to the woman this girl would become? Or was it simply a moment captured of a girl born into the Victorian era, cossetted by a country idyll, enjoying the leafy surroundings of her childhood world? Life for Nancy Tennant did indeed begin in this way.

Born in 1897, she was the adored youngest of William Augustus Tennant and Agnes Hannah Gairdner's four children. Ernest, born in 1887, was the eldest, followed by Charles Alan, who was known as 'Bunny'. The third child was the beautiful and vivacious Margaret who was seven years older than Nancy. In many ways the Tennants appeared to be typical of a comfortably-off, upper-middle class English family. They lived at Orford House in Ugley, an early eighteenth-century manor built by the 1st Earl of Orford, surrounded by the acres of land that went with it. This was Essex, a place of winding lanes, big skies and chocolate box thatched cottages in the decades before any urban sprawl reached it. With a resident staff, comprising a cook, a parlour maid, a housemaid and a gardener to see to all the domestic chores, the family were free to indulge in leisure pursuits. They played lawn tennis and croquet and had tea parties in the shade of a large cedar tree, with the solid silver teapot and scones keeping warm in a chafing dish, in proper Edwardian fashion. Hunting, shooting and country pastimes were order of the day, while the Home Farm, orchards and vegetable gardens kept the kitchens well supplied with fresh produce.

Yet the Tennants weren't really English at all. The clue was in the surname. Flowing through their veins, on both parents' sides, ran strong, no-nonsense Scottish blood. Not the blood of aristocratic Catholics and flamboyant Dukes north of the border, but gritty, lowland, crofting blood which only a century and a half earlier had worked its way out of the glens to create one of the greatest fortunes in the industrialised world.

In Simon Blow's 'Broken Blood', The Rise and the Fall of the Tennant Family,' he explains how the first flush of industrial creativity for the family hinged on the growth of the linen trade in Scotland. 'By the 1770's Scotland had 252 factories in operation, with Glasgow as the linen capital, producing 2 million yards of cloth per year.' The founding father of the Tennant fortunes was the energetic and largely self-educated Charles. At the age of 15 he left his rural existence behind and became an apprentice weaver in Kilbarchan, a village near Paisley. It was significant and lucky that he was near Paisley. The town had become the innovative and intellectually enlightened weaving capital of Scotland and was a mecca for ambitious Scots making their way in the textile industry. Tennant, as a Paisley apprentice transformed from a lowly crofter facing a future of scratching a living from the land, to being an educated skilled worker who could not only read and write, but potentially set up his own business if he was ambitious enough. Bleaching linen, and later cotton, lay at the heart of the success of the industry and the basic chemistry required to do so had remained unchanged for centuries. Whilst England had its wool trade, France and Scotland turned to the manufacture of linen and cotton. There was much cross-pollination of ideas not only in chemical and industrial innovation between France and Scotland, but also in politics and ideas of social restructuring.

Charles eventually moved on to Glasgow. With the useful presence of a French bookshop in the city, young Charles Tennant not only taught himself French, but taught himself chemistry in French. In his twenties, he bought bleach fields, in partnership with a friend, and became consumed with revolutionising the chemistry of the linen trade, which to date involved spreading linen out in the fields for days to turn white. He recognised that if he could create the perfect compound, it would set him apart, and ahead. His determination and industrious application paid off and he finally alighted on an innovative formula. An almost inconceivable industrial success would begin to gain traction not only for his company, but for Glasgow too. Within a few decades, his company, Tennant Knox & Co, would lead the way in bleach production at St Rollox Bleaching Salt Works in Glasgow. He never forgot his humble roots. He was a member of the Friends of the People and an admirer of Thomas Paine who called for the abolition of all titles. He was a liberal thinker and a Radical. By his death, in 1838, he had established a sizeable fortune worth several million pounds in today's money. But it was his grandson, Sir Charles Tennant, knighted by the Prime Minister, William Gladstone, who was the equivalent of a tech company billionaire. Coupling a brilliant education with an ability to see that the fusion of Empire, trade links and innovation could take the bleach business global, his expansion worldwide not only resulted in his children and their descendants marrying into the grandest families in the land, it enabled wealth to be spread around the further reaches of the family. Nancy's family descended from Sir Charles Tennant's uncle William, who was tasked with setting up C Tennant Sons & Co as the company headquarters in London.

Nancy's immediate family were by all accounts, kind and warm hearted. Letters between siblings and parents', grandparents, aunts and uncles reveal an informal affection (in spite of their habit of using their surnames to sign off even letters to their children). The cornerstone of the family unit was her parents' very genuine affection, respect and admiration for each other. Educated in what had become the Tennant family tradition at Eton and then Cambridge, William Tennant met and fell madly in love with the exquisitely pretty and feminine Agnes Gairdner, a school friend of his sister, Molly. She was, according to him, "a bit of a flirt then and behaved in this way rather to test me out." He proposed to her a year after they first met "one Sunday afternoon on the top of a half-built haystack."

Agnes Gairdner hailed from a charmed, Scottish, lowland background. The daughter of a Glasgow banker and an energetic, enthusiastic mother, she was brought up in a large happy family at Broom House near Glasgow. Described by her younger sister, Lucy Gairdner, in her memoirs, Broom House was a '*large house standing in fields and with a pond which was the joy of our hearts, as we had a little rowing boat, HMS Pinafore, in which we spent very many happy hours and learnt how to row . . . we also learnt to skate there, led by Mother who was always a pioneer in sports, which were not then thought to be quite ladylike. My father added on to the house a billiard room and schoolroom with nurseries above them and there was always a staff of about 11 servants who must have had a busy time.*' Lucy recollects a happy childhood of governesses, dancing classes and a sense of pride in being the first girls to introduce hockey to Scotland. Whether that is true or not, their mother was open-minded to suitable activities for her daughters. They finished their education in Brussels at a finishing school, 'Miss Anderson's' where they spent two years perfecting their language skills.

Lucy goes on to describe her sister's wedding: *the first wedding in the family was Agnes's to Will Tennant on 27th July 1886 and it made a great stir as it took place in the drawing-room at Broom and a large party was invited. A marquee was erected on the lawn outside the French window and a sit-down lunch for . . . 100 guests was provided. It was the beginning of a very happy connection with the Tennant family and Anna [another sister] married Jack Tennant 10 years later in the same room'.*

Agnes's mother, Hannah McNair's sense of independent thinking wasn't just confined to gender appropriate sport. She encouraged her daughters to challenge the political status-quo. The adult Lucy Gairdner worked as a secretary to the Queen Margaret Settlement in Glasgow, an institution that promoted social welfare, particularly for impoverished women and children. She counted its founder, the Suffragette, Mary Anderson Snodgrass, the daughter of a flour miller as one of her greatest friends and influences. The seeds of the acceptability of independent minded women in the family were sown and nurtured by Hannah, long before her granddaughter Nancy began to think for herself as an adult.

There was no doubt Nancy enjoyed music from a young age but stewing away like a Regency maiden until she was of marriageable age in Essex was not what William and Agnes had in mind for the education of their youngest child. After a few formative years with 'a tall, dismal governess' she was sent to live with Gairdner relations in Glasgow: her Uncle Charlie, Aunt Bea and their daughter, Una. Education for girls really mattered for the Tennant family.

'I learned more in those two years than at any other time in my life,' she reflected later. *'Every morning Una and I set off on a twenty-minute uphill walk to join about eight other girls for a class presided over by a Miss Sturrock.'* Nancy was riveted by her teacher who had not only black beady eyes but a black moustache. She commanded total respect

and ignited her pupils' interests. *'Every subject came to life, especially geography. We put on imaginary bonnets and set off for trips abroad. Milan Cathedral seemed an old friend when I saw it years later.'*

The power of music and its effect on the human psyche impressed her for the first time in her lessons with a piano teacher. Una's mother had persuaded a young organist from Glasgow University to teach the two giggling girl cousins. "He had long carroty hair and a fiery temperament to match," Nancy said, "Una and my efforts to play our pieces were more than he could stand: we were shoved off the piano stool and he settled down to play himself." Exasperated by the ineptitude of his pupils he may have been, but thanks to the young organist, Nancy witnessed the transformative power of music being more than a genteel accomplishment. Nancy was always modest about her own musical ability but it was significant and obvious to those around her. After a fallow couple of years at a boarding school in Malvern, "where I learned absolutely nothing except a lot of French," the two cousins were sent to Paris to develop their language skills and in Nancy's case improve her singing and study music properly. She was following a well-trodden path. She was being 'finished' before being launched into the marriage market at the age of seventeen. But rather than taking private lessons, in the autumn of 1914, she entered the hallowed doors of the Paris Conservatoire and studied music alongside the major talents of the time.

By the early 20th century the Paris Conservatoire was a melting pot of excellence, creativity and musical ambition. When Nancy arrived, Igor Stravinsky's successful partnership with Sergei Diaghilev would have been at its height, with Le Ballets Russes performing *The Firebird* and *The Rite of Spring* to enthralled audiences. Gabriel Fauré was the director of the Paris Conservatoire; Ravel, Debussy and Saint-Saëns were its alumni. To a young, musical enthusiast it was eye opening. Anything was possible, Nancy thought, and music could, after all, be her career and the cornerstone of who she might become. But it was 1914, and within weeks of arriving in Paris, she was made to return home. War had been declared.

CHAPTER THREE

A Glorious, Hot Summer

1914

*'Nothing in life shall sever the chain
that is round us now.'*

When Gavrilo Princip fired the fatal shot at Archduke Franz Ferdinand one sunny Sarajevo day on Saturday 28th June 1914, it was inconceivable that it would trigger a chain of events that would lead to World War One and the mass destruction of a generation of young men. Until then, as far as meeting an eligible suitor went, Nancy had been born with every advantage. Moving seamlessly from the Victorian age of prurience to the Edwardian era of elegance and worldliness, with the advantage of wealth, intellectual ability and musical talent, she might have been, in a different, parallel 20th century, tailor made for her time, an exemplary wife. She wasn't the belle of the ball by any means, her sister Margaret was the acknowledged beauty in the family, but she was witty, kind and talented and moreover had plenty of family money behind her to ensure a happy match with a well-educated, comfortably off young man. She also had a promising musical career ahead. Her voice was good enough for professional singing.

The doomed generation of young officer class men she might have married, she described later in her life as "a flowery lot". By flowery she wasn't speaking in code about the sexuality of Wilfred Owen, Rupert Brooke and Siegfried Sassoon, she meant the equally brilliant aristocrats such as Ego and Yvo Charteris, Julian and Billy Grenfell and Patrick Shaw-Stewart. Their creed was based on patriotism, the romantic ideal and scholarship - the pursuit of knowledge for its own sake rather than a means to financial security or an academic career. "They were a very splendid lot. They came from very flowery backgrounds. You realise the wealth of the Edwardian life, the background of culture. They were a class apart in a way" said Nancy, but that was in hindsight.

In the meantime, the summer sun of 1914 blazing in the Balkans on that June day, also shone over England for the entire week and into the following weekend. It was perfect weather for outdoor picnics and socialising. Nancy was growing up and beginning to have fun. "The summer was heavenly. I was still in bud, not at all pretty but good at singing. 1914 was my first Henley Regatta. On the way to it our car broke down. A gypsy appeared who insisted on telling our fortunes. I was told I should marry Archie Middleton, a school friend of my brother, Ernest, who was with us in the party."

Henley Royal Regatta would have been a perfect introduction to formal social occasions for her. It was a high point in the Season every year, especially for a family like the Tennants who were keen oarsmen. A fluttering pageant of striped blazers, boaters, feminine dresses and hats: schoolboys and undergraduates starring in the races with team spirits riding high. Picnics were served from large wicker baskets, with finely sliced cucumber sandwiches, anchovy paste and potted shrimps. Glasses of iced Camp Coffee were glugged gratefully down, the sweet, chicory flavoured old fashioned version of a milk shake being a distinctive feature of the Henley drinks menu. The tone of the gathering was gentler, more Home Counties; it wasn't the raffish mix of society grandees, racetrack punters and huge sums of money lost and won, as at Royal Ascot. Henley was more like a private club (or a collection of private clubs like the Leander which hosted the regatta) of England's top public schools and oldest Oxbridge colleges. Many of the boys and young men rowing in the boats and socialising at picnics and on the banks of the Thames would become machine gun fodder in a matter of months. By the end of 1915, most of the men in the Tennant picnic party at Henley, including Archie Middleton, were dead.

Much has been written about the delusion and subsequent suffering of First World War but less is mentioned about the explosion of euphoria at the start of it. The image of Kitchener pointing, declaring 'Your Country Needs YOU' that 21st century schoolchildren are shown, gave no indication of the level of public excitement at the prospect. As Ego (Hugo) Charteris, the son of the Earl of Wemyss and leading exponent of the flowery patriotism Nancy had described, wrote: '*The fighting-excitement vitalizes everything, every sight and action. One loves one's fellow man so much more when one is bent on killing him.*' Quite apart from the upper-classes' enthusiasm for combat was the use of atrocity propaganda by British government – like the Kitchener poster - which very effectively mobilized public opinion in favour of 'crushing the Hun.' So much so that in Germany in the 1920's, former military leaders like Erich Ludendorff suggested that British propaganda had been instrumental in their defeat. Adolf Hitler echoed that view, and the Nazis later used many British propaganda techniques during their time in power.

The first member of the Tennant family to head off to battle was Margaret's husband, Archie Mercer. The couple had married in 1913, having met on a passenger boat to Canada where Margaret, with her parents, was sailing out to visit her brother Bunny who was working in Montreal. Despite outward appearances Margaret and Archie were captivated by each other. Archie was solemn and bookish with neat, dark hair, glasses and a trim moustache. Margaret, pretty and viva-cious, was fifteen years his junior. *'I suppose her chief charm is her delightfully sunny disposition with a really very clever brain,'* wrote Archie to his parents, telling them of their engagement. They married in Ugley Church in August 1913 and set sail for a life in Poona, India immediately afterwards.

Like Nancy, Margaret had inherited her family's trait of inde-pendent, liberal thinking and found the racism and societal division of colonial India hard to accept. Befriending local Parsee women, she openly challenged the social status quo of British Raj to the surprise of her husband's army friends. By the late spring of 1914, she was expecting their first child. She chose to return to England and made her way to Orford House to sit out the final weeks of her confine-ment. She was not well. She had lost weight, was jaundiced, horrifying her sixteen-year-old sister when she returned home to Essex. *'I have never forgotten the shock of seeing my darling sister, who had gone away so blooming and beautiful, yellow and emaciated with jaundice, almost unrecognisable,'* wrote Nancy. Archie had not accompanied his wife home to England, as his regiment was required in Basra. He waited for news of the arrival of his first born.

Nancy's brother, Alan, the younger of the two Tennant brothers, was desperate to enlist and fight for 'King and Country' along with his two first cousins from Glasgow and was returning from Montreal to join up. Charles Alan Tennant, known as 'Bunny' was a gilded youth. He had none of the responsibilities that his elder brother Ernest was expected to assume but all the advantages of good looks, a first-class education and a secure future. After leaving school, he was sent to Canada to work for Charles Tennant & Co in Montreal. It would have been an exciting adventure, a good place for a young man to cut his teeth in business and try out an independent life. Montreal at the turn of the century was a broiling pit of male ambi-tion and mass immigration. The city's population swelled accordingly, with factories and industry springing up like mushrooms. Ernest

Tennant thought it fairly dingy when he first visited in November 1911 and stayed in the Windsor Hotel in the city. He wrote:

'A terrible collection of blackguards seems always [to be] standing in the hall. Everyone is talking dollars and big business. Spitoons are everywhere. There is one beside every chair and there is perpetual expectoration . . . the huge and rather beautiful dining room is without a carpet because of this spitting habit. There are many fine buildings in Montreal but the effect is ruined by the filthiness of the streets, which are most squalid . . .'. But for young Bunny it was an invigorating environment and he relished the challenge.

The moment war was declared, he determined to return to England as quickly as he could and enlist. *'He was really frightened he would miss it, he said 'we are fighting for the forces of Christ against the forces of evil'*' wrote Nancy. He joined the London Scottish Regiment, trained with them for three months and then, in March 1915, kissed his parents and sisters goodbye and left for the Front. As William Tennant waved off his youngest son he had a sinking feeling he would never see him again. He was right. Within a matter of weeks, Second Lieutenant Tennant had been killed. His regiment, the Dorsetshire, was one of the first to move on the 9th May in the Battle of Aubers Ridge. It was a disaster. Poor intelligence combined with limited and badly made ammunition ensured German victory.

Later reports confirmed that, on the eve of the Battle of Aubers Ridge, Bunny and his platoon had taken their positions in hidden trenches about a mile and a half behind the front line. The Artillery began their bombardment at 5am. It was clear, sunny weather and everyone was in good spirits. At first the platoon ran through some orchards, with one shell exploding near Bunny. He was, according to those who fought alongside 'visibly shaken' by it but not hurt. The company ran through a gateway and made its dash. *'it was pretty evident that the enemy had both machine and big guns trained on the spot, for it was thick with bodies when we arrived,'* Bunny's surviving Platoon Sergeant, James Duffy wrote, *'Mr Tennant went first and I followed. We had gone about a dozen yards when a huge shell burst close to us almost blinding me with smoke . . . and then I saw him lying just behind, so I ran back and dropped down by his side. He was lying quite naturally on his face and I couldn't see any wounds, but when I asked him where he was hit, the only reply was "shell," and "get on, take charge", and then no reply at all. Concluding that he was either stunned or dead, I had to go on and, in his absence, take charge of the platoon but from what I have heard from others I do not think he ever moved again. I need not trouble you with any more details. Unfortunately, I was unable to get to him any more as I was hit myself, but have been told by one of those who helped to pick him up that no wounds were found, and it was considered that he must have been killed by the concussion of the shell, or else died of shock.'*

The battle lasted just over a month and was declared a German victory on 18th June. It was a disaster for the British. It achieved zero strategic value at the expense of 32,000 casualties. Bunny Tennant was buried in the land in which he fell. There was no medal or record of bravery as consolation, he was just another wasted young life in the muddy mess.

For Nancy, the world was beginning to turn on a very miserable axis. The heat, flirtations and happiness of the summer were a mere ten months away, but her future was crumbling before her, and beyond her worst imaginings.

'I look back on the first week in May 1915 as being the time when I was catapulted from adolescence into adulthood. All the family were away, Father in America, Mother in Scotland where Granny was dying, Margaret nursing in Weymouth. I had two Tennant cousins staying, Sheena and Meg. It was perfect spring weather. We picnicked in the bluebells. On Tuesday morning Meg went back to London and that evening I was rung by Sheena's sister in Scotland asking me to tell Sheena that their brother Charlie had been killed. Meg had the same news about her brother the same day. At lunchtime the telephone rang and a voice read out a telegram regretting that Alan Tennant had been killed. Just

before I left for London to stay with my brother Ernest, another letter arrived for Mother from Bunny with 'only to be sent if I am killed' on the envelope.

'Dearest Mother We are in for a very big fight tomorrow, so I am going to leave this note in my pocket and it will only get to you if I am knocked out. I just want to say Good-bye, Mother dear, I have had a very happy time of it, and the nicest lot of near relatives that a man was ever blessed with.

Don't feel sorry for me; it is not everyone who had the privilege of dying for all he thinks worthwhile in the world, and this old world without British influence for good and without you dear people would be a poor place to live in. We are fighting for very high ideals, justice, honesty, fair play among nations; for the teachings of Christ as against those of the devil. It is an unselfish cause and one for which I am very proud to be fighting. I know you will be sad. I would not have it otherwise, but you can comfort yourself by the thought that you, too have had to make a sacrifice for the noblest possible cause. Your very loving son, Alan'.

CHAPTER FOUR

Deadly Peace

1916

'I remember a deadly sense of peace coming over me when I realised I didn't think I knew anyone else left to be killed.'

The ceaseless, driving rain associated with trench warfare was not simply a cinematic device used by film directors to reinforce the misery of the First World War. The wet winter of 1914 through to February 1915 in Northern Europe was real and long. On the 19th November 1914, the news reached Margaret Mercer at Orford House that her husband had been killed in Iraq. Ten days later, with rain still hammering down from a leaden Essex sky, she went into labour. Traumatised and bereaved, aware her child would never know its father, she feared she would die in the process. But Margaret, who believed "that any admission of feeling unwell was a regrettable state of moral weakness" survived. She gave birth to a daughter on the 30th November. They named her Ariel after her father's middle name. In spite of the jaundice Margaret had suffered during the early stages of pregnancy, and in spite of the terrible tragedy leading up to her birth, the baby girl "was undamaged and strong and the only light in the darkness."

Beyond the joy of the new baby, the months that followed were bleak, reaching a terrible crescendo of despair when the news of Bunny's death arrived. Nancy described her mother, descending into frequent depressive episodes as "shattered with grief". Her father, who was contributing in his capacity as an experienced businessman, co-ordinating the production and distribution of weapons, for the Ministry of Munitions during the war, was more stoic. He had been visiting the Tennant offices in New York when the grim news arrived. He telegrammed his family saying, "For now we see through a glass darkly, but then face to face". His acceptance of adversity followed by hope for the future was an attempt at consolation but in May 1915, their world, for the time being, was very dark indeed.

Nancy used the word "mercifully" liberally. She often applied the phrase "God moves in mysterious ways" to otherwise tragic events. Her father's reference to One Corinthians in his attempt to console his family at their most unhappy hour, remained with her throughout her life. She felt it helped her to accept that, at a time of great suffering, the present is unfathomable and the future is unknowable; that not having to understand *why* terrible events occurred was a form of relief in itself. She applied "God's mysterious ways" to the fortunate survival of her eldest brother who could not be conscripted. As a former tuberculosis patient, Ernest was unable to fight but his absence from combat left him no less traumatised and angry about the decimation of his generation. Fluent in German, he eventually found a position in intelligence. He wrote: '*It was not until 1916 that I was accepted for service, in the Intelligence Corps, and 1917 before I got to France. By then I no longer regretted not having been accepted in 1914, for the war had become a shambles and most of my friends and relatives of combatant age had already been killed.*'

Of Ernest's immediate group of school friends (there were twenty-eight), nineteen were dead by 1916. In addition, Bunny had volunteered the staff of the Tennant's young Montreal office who were all killed in 1915. The office never reopened. *'Of my combatant Tennant relations, brother and cousins, out of eleven of military age, seven had been killed by the time I was passed fit for service. The men of my generation, many of whom would have been directing the Commonwealth, and probably the world today were almost wiped out within four years at Loos, at Ypres, in Gallipoli, in Mesopotamia, on the Somme, at Passchendaele, and on the sea and in the air.'*

And yet the world kept turning. Nancy found the cycle of the seasons, continuing to revolve regardless of human misery, almost unbearable. She and her mother attempted a change of scene with a visit to Archie's brother-in-law in Weymouth, whom she described as a quiet shy man, who was an unforgettable support to them all. But so soon after so much bereavement, the otherwise restorative sight of waves crashing on the shore was too much to bear. *'I came to hate the sight of the sea, going so remorselessly in and out, in and out, while our world crumbled.'*

As Nancy and her mother walked along the town's seafront, their eyes would have alighted on more than the breaking waves. Weymouth was the designated convalescent town for injured and recovering ANZAC troops from Gallipoli. Over 120,000 injured soldiers passed through town, recovered from their injuries and once fit, were sent off to fight again. From early 1915, the distinctive Hospital Blue uniform used by convalescent soldiers, indicating they were capable of getting out of bed, was a common sight on the seafront. Some walked unaided, taking the air, or for those less fortunate, pushed along the pavement in wheelchairs by their fellow soldiers. Reminders of Bunny's final weeks and subsequent death were everywhere.

As war work seemed the best place to channel her energy and grief, Margaret resolved to leave Ariel with her mother and sister and go to France. Her early widowhood could have reduced her to a self-pitying post-natal wreck, but somehow the combination of an Edwardian upbringing and Scottish grit kicked in. She felt compelled to help and signed up with a casualty clearing station in Reims. The photograph on her French Red Cross Medal Card is revealing. The beautiful, vivacious young woman who had met Archie Mercer on the boat to Canada, looks dirty and exhausted but defiantly determined as she glares at the camera.

Once she had returned from Weymouth, Nancy was tasked with making calico bags for soldiers. It was lonely and dull and although she had a sewing-machine she was bad at it, claiming to sew more fingers than successful bags. The Paris Conservatoire faded into a distant memory. "Music was irrelevant when every day brought news of more disasters".

In the autumn 1915, an Artillery Brigade arrived in Stanstead and Nancy was asked to work in the YMCA. In later years she described it dismissively as "all very decorous and ladylike, handing out cups of tea" but it was the start of a new direction. The woman who supervised her was the 'rather silly' Mrs Myrea but she was cheerful and proactive. Within a few weeks, she had asked Nancy to join her working in a canteen she was due to run on Salisbury Plain. ANZAC troops had arrived at Tidworth, a new camp had been built and they needed young women to volunteer with its cleaning and management.

Nancy accepted the job and, in the winter 1917, left home. There was camaraderie amongst the handful of eighteen-year-old girls who now had a purpose. Their living conditions were almost comically tough, based on the idea they should experience similar discomfort to the troops in the trenches. They slept in a large hut which leaked when it rained and had no heating. Nancy caught the dripping rainwater in a bowl on her bed. Tasks included scrubbing the floors and 'heaving' kit bags around. There was singing too and the girls put on plays together. "I had some success as Portia and even more as Charley's real Aunt." But beneath the friendships and activity ran an undercurrent of dread. For all the cheer and vigour, the troops were stationed at the camp for one thing only. They were all due to leave for battle. With a sinking heart Nancy watched the never-ending columns of marching soldiers, singing "It's A Long, Long Trail Awinding' as they moved off. Over 60,000 Anzac troops died in the First World War.

Salisbury Plain in winter is a bleak, alien landscape, its grassy undulations rolling relentlessly into the distance. For Nancy, bereaved, tired and disorientated it felt as welcoming as the moon. For her, cheering off the troops, the same age as her now dead brother, cousins and brothers' friends eventually took its toll. The teenaged girl who had set foot so confidently in Paris with her cousin Una, had now lived an entirely different reality. In the 21st century she would most likely have been diagnosed with PTSD, as she described the atmosphere at the barracks as "highly charged". Her parents, who were uncomfortable about her being there, probably anticipated what was coming next. After a few months, she described herself as "cracking up completely". It was time to return home to Essex and become a Land Girl.

There were far worse fates to befall a young Edwardian woman than finding herself leaning comfortably against the warm flank of a dairy cow while she milked it, but the change in Nancy's life from promenading the elegant boulevards of Paris to mucking out an Essex cattleshed - in three short years - was seismic. The Tennants had their own farm and dairy herd, so being a Land Girl simply required her to join the other members of the Women's Land Army who were already at work. There was plenty of political encouragement, if not pressure, as the excellent government propaganda machine got underway. Posters, featuring resolute and astonishingly pretty young women, ploughing the land with horse-drawn ploughs as the sun rose over the fields, were embellished with jingoistic slogans: "God speed the Plough and the Woman who Drives it" read one, "Get Behind the Girl he left Behind" demanded another.

An aspect which greatly influenced women's fashion forevermore, was the Land Girls' clothing. As it was impossible to work wearing long dresses and frilly Edwardian clothing, these young women adapted tight masculine riding boots, jodhpurs, working men's jackets and even dungarees, to fit them. Every woman, regardless of her background, had to wear the same and this rule cut across class boundaries for the first time. The work itself required everyone to pitch in, regardless, but Nancy, although used to servants and domestic comfort, generally found it satisfying. In the absence of Nancy's father, who was in America working for the Ministry of Munitions, her widowed aunt was given the responsibility of running the Orford home farm. The aunt was rather clever, had taken an agricultural degree at Reading and taught Nancy how to make butter and cheese. "I liked milking and working in the fields," she said, "but making butter was repetitive and dull and I found it jolly boring." It can't have been lost on Nancy that through her experience as a Land Girl, far from being the fairer sex, ready to take instruction from men, women from all backgrounds were more than able to do what had hitherto been regarded as 'men's work' and moreover, be organised in doing it. As each Land Girl took up her tools, ploughed the fields, scrubbed the dairies clean and mucked out the animals, she was one individual in a workforce of thousands. A workforce which would have a far mightier role to play when the grim years of the war were finally over.

CHAPTER FIVE

Finding Purpose

1919

*'Our generation were never young – we didn't have that sort
of youth – we had to pick ourselves up but never again was
there that carefree sense.'*

At the stroke of eleven on 11th November 1918, London's damp
morning air filled with sound. Whistles screamed, horns blew,
church bells rang all over the city and in the country beyond it. Maroon
rockets, usually a warning of approaching German bombers, flashed
brightly, blasting into the sky. Bonfires were lit, street parties began and
a euphoric wave of jubilation swept through the war worn population.

Nancy's father was already at the offices at C Tennant & Son in
London and summoned his family up from Essex to witness the
elation. For Nancy it felt bizarre to celebrate a generation of doomed
youth. *'I was most unwilling, it all seemed too late and too sad,'* she
wrote. But she was persuaded to go and conceded that the positively
charged jubilation of the crowds was infectious. *'It was a wonderful
experience to stand among the milling crowd, cheering the King and*

Queen as they came out onto the balcony of Buckingham Palace. The one thing that sustained people was that it was the war to end all wars.'

Little by little, life picked up. As Nancy's work as a Land Girl ceased, her social life re-emerged. Margaret returned from working in France and moved into a house in Kensington which she shared with their father William, during the week. Ernest, his wife Noni and their growing family also set up home in London where a version of pre-war routine began to establish itself. Domestic staff, having returned from their war efforts, continued to be integral to the smooth running of grand and middle-class households under the assumption that the status quo was intact. Socialising followed the same pre-war conventions of the London Season in summer with all its lavish entertainments, followed by country house parties and then North in August to Yorkshire and Scotland for the field sports.

The Edwardian habit of paying visits, which meant staying with friends or relations for weeks at a time, or having groups of friends and relations to stay at your own country house after the London Season was over, was a familiar rite of passage for Nancy. A visit required extensive packing of clothes, which were changed several times a day. Different outfits were worn in the morning, at lunch, at tea, for dinner and dances, not to mention full tweed for shooting or a bespoke riding habit for hunting. But for Nancy, the social round proved profoundly lonely. Gone was the flutter of romantic expectation of who may or may not be staying for a long weekend, because there were few, if any, young suitors to sit next to at dinner or a summer picnic. Because of the gaping holes left by the war in the fabric of her generation, the expectation that she would fall in love and live happily ever after was receding fast.

She felt estranged by her war experiences from the blithe spirits of her teenage years. She explained: *'My generation was never young, we didn't have that sort of youth. Some became 'young' when the war was over, there was an explosion of the roaring 20's, that sort of thing, but we weren't in that. We didn't have that sort of regeneration. We had to pick ourselves up but never again was there that carefree sense. We had to put away childish things too suddenly and I remember thinking that I should never feel really young again. I see myself [then] as ponderously proper, rather plain, badly dressed not at all the magnet for admirers.'*

In spite of how she saw herself, she knew she had plenty of friends, was secure in her parents' love and had, in Bunny's words, "the nicest lot of near relatives". Her cousins provided another layer of familiar, family security. There was no doubt that Nancy adored her mother. She felt and bore witness to her mother's profound sense of loss after the death of her brother in the war. *'She never fully recovered from the shock of Bunny's death, totally uninterested in food, she had to plan three meals a day for the family, constant visitors, to say nothing of servants. We had cooked breakfast, three course lunch, huge tea and then four or five course dinner, for which she every evening wrote menus.'* The voids that could never be filled and those who should have occupied the voids had vanished. Packing trunks with clothes for ceaseless socialising was not enough. Nancy needed to find meaningful work and Agnes Tennant needed something more than focussing on domestic matters.

In the years that immediately followed the end of the war, memorial crosses and 'memorial halls' were an increasingly common sight in villages and towns across the country. After the loss of his son, his son-in-law and the sons of families in the village, as lord of the manor, William Tennant felt it was his responsibility to build a war memorial and a memorial hall at Ugley. He opened their village hall in 1921. *'My parents were, in a way, parents to the village. People were so helpless in those days . . . you could get turned out of your house at the end of the week, and if your husband got ill, there was nothing behind you . . . my parents felt responsible for the welfare of the village. My father was a very ardent Liberal and the idea of being called a Squire was something that would send him into a real fury,'* wrote Nancy.

William Tennant's liberal values included a belief in the education of girls and women. He passionately supported both his daughters and in later years, his granddaughter, Ariel, in all their endeavours and took their interests and views seriously. Where memorial halls had been built, there was now a new community focal point in every village that wasn't either the pub or the Church. Critically, it was a place where women could go, simply to meet each other for any reason at all, whether practical or social. God, alcohol and men were not required. Women and their sense of self mattered to him and he respected their independence of mind.

Once the village hall had been built, Agnes saw an opportunity. A new 'Movement' for women had arrived from Canada and she decided to start a branch of her own.

'My mother started the WI in Ugley in 1921. For the first time we had somewhere where we could meet.' When Nancy wrote 'we' she was not referring to women of her background, she was talking about all women, regardless of their education, wealth or position.

By 1921, the Women's Institute had gathered momentum in England and Wales. Decades before the caricature of bossy matrons competitively presiding over cake and jam production became the cliché, the 'National Federation of Women's Institutes' held a lofty and radical ambition. Founded in Canada at the end of the 19th century, it was conceived as a counterpoint to the effects of industrialisation on rural communities, the loss of crafts, values and way of life. Most importantly it also sought to give rural women the voice they were beginning to dare to use during the war years and provide a sense of mutual support. Viewed through a 21st century lens, it is easy to regard what appeared to be do-goodery as almost quaint, verging on genteel virtue-signalling by privileged middle England women. But in the early 1920's, before most women were able to vote, giving rural women a sense of self-determination and independence was revolutionary. *'As women generally play so important a part in the work of a farm, they should have an organisation of their own which would enable them to do what they could to advance the welfare of both home life and of agriculture.'* (The Organisation of Agriculture in England and Other Lands, Edwin Pratt, Village Voices.)

Rural life and the economic realities of farming at the close of the 19th century were tough. Cheaper European food imports and the Government's decision to put sterling back on the Gold Standard resulted in a profound drop in economic security and even viability for rural communities. The days of a farmer's life being comfortable and materially secure were over and their wives were the ones who suffered most. The focus was not on the wives of fairly comfortable gentlemen farmers who might have farmed vast swathes of land attached to big estates, it was on the smallholders; farmers who occupied a traditional small farmhouse and farmyard. Tied to these small farmsteads, rural women were expected to pull their weight at home and on the land, often in isolated locations. With an absence of domestic appliances, electricity and even running water for some homes, the labour was relentless. The women who had married before the war and were now raising young families were particularly affected. The class system kept them ground down further. No vote, no economic freedom, no contraception and certainly no voice, the idea of being mistresses of their own lives was unimaginable.

~

In 1913, a young widow, Margaret Watt, founder member of the Canadian Women's Institute Movement arrived in England ostensibly to complete her sons' education. She was also determined to introduce the success of the Canadian WI to Britain. An academic, writer and activist, she was convinced that if women worked collectively it would give them greater power. She was dismayed by what she found in the resigned apathy of the female rural community. "I was disgusted," she reported back, "the women sat silent and took no part in discussions . . . they sat there like oysters!" But Madge (as Margaret liked to be known), didn't give up. She was determined to empower women through egalitarian social groups which would educate, inform and support all women regardless of class and education, allowing them to take control of their lives on the most basic and fundamental of levels.

~

So it was that the Government backed Agricultural Organisations Society became her springboard; this was the body that had funded the women's Land Army, and was now possessed of a network that could be utilized for the creation of a movement for women. Finding local leadership was hard. The Canadian model had to adapt to the class structure of Britain where a feudal system still operated in the countryside as far as women and their influence went. Just as upper-class social life remained Edwardian, the medieval concept of *noblesse oblige* was the way the English Womens' Institute found its English leaders. Poorly educated, rural women had no idea they could have a voice, let alone have it heard. It was the wives of the landed, rich and influential who would have to take the baton and run with it on their behalf.

~

Privileged as the early pioneers and leaders of the WI may have been, they sprinkled the largesse of their influence equally among their members and the effect they had was just as significant as that of the Suffragettes. Some of the founding members had been suffragists and members of suffrage societies. '*The Institutes were in some sense the rural counterpart of the banding together of women in the urban areas, in a common fight for freedom and independence of thought and action.*' Although the Representation of the People Bill had been passed in 1918 giving property-owning women over the age of 30 the right to vote it wasn't until 1928, that all women were legally allowed to vote, regardless of their economic or marital status. Agnes Tennant was exactly the sort of woman the NFWI (National Federation of Women's Institutes) needed to start a group but Agnes also needed a secretary. She asked Nancy to take the position and her daughter accepted.

CHAPTER SIX

Travel and Music

The bonfire in a clearing in the snowy Austrian woods crackled and spat. It was a relief to stand close to it. Bowls of spicy *Gulasch* were handed out to the assembled group of grateful men and women. After a long, cold morning in pony carts, bumping through the woods from one shooting stand to another, the food and fire were a welcome source of comfort. The shooting party had met for lunch, forming a circle around the flames. It was a glamorous and international gathering of Viennese aristocracy, bankers and business men. Nancy's companion that morning had been a man of immense charm and film star good looks. The thirty-eight year old Baron Louis de Rothschild and Miss Tennant had woven their way through the woods together on a little pony drawn *barouche*. Stopping at intervals, waiting for a hare to appear or not, taking aim, then re-embarking and continuing the activity. Nancy remembered his elegance and chivalry decades later, "wrapping me up in his lovely black cloak" against the cold winter air. None of this party of Jewish bankers, Austrian grandees and English aristocrats could have guessed that this gilded, cosmopolitan world would be entirely destroyed in the following decade. By 1939, Hitler had invaded Austria, declared himself ruler in the *Anschluss* and Louis de Rothschild was imprisoned by the Nazis.

His story would prove to be the most dramatic. As a member of the powerful Rothschild banking dynasty, he had been brought up in a world of immense family wealth, culture and social status. Emperor Francis II awarded the hereditary title of Baron to the Vienna branch of the family in acknowledgement of the financial support they had given the Austrian government. The Austrian Rothschild branch was regarded by the European ruling classes as one of their own, particularly as it bankrolled so much of the economy. However, in 1938, the Rothschilds' art-filled palaces in Vienna, known collectively as Palais Rothschild, were seized in the *Anschluss* and their contents confiscated. Hitler had plans to create the greatest collection of European art as part of his new order. Attempting to flee from Austria in 1938, Louis was arrested by the Nazis at Aspern airport and imprisoned, until a ransom, reputedly of twenty-one million dollars, was paid after a year. He was to spend the rest of his life in exile.

But on that day in 1921, under the bright, clear skies of eastern Europe, the *Gulasch* and the company were joyful and stimulating. Nancy, on holiday from her duties at the WI, was touring Europe with new friends, Michael and Penelope Spencer-Smith, a couple who had recently moved to Ugley and taken her under their wing. "Penny was musical and we quickly made friends. It was a friendship that brought many changes and much happiness into my life."

Music was by now firmly back at the centre of Nancy's life. Her teenage dreams of living as a Parisian music student at the Conservatoire were now a thing of the past but her parents were happy to support her closer to home. Spending the week with maiden Gairdner aunts in a house in Kensington gave her access to some of the best singing teachers and choral musicians in the world. The teachers ranged from intimidating to indulgent. She was so frightened of her first, reputedly "best teacher in London" that she found even walking up to her front door in Queensgate petrifying, pacing up and down past the grand stucco villas, a bag of nerves, delaying the moment of entry. It didn't last. Her next teacher was a soulful Russian woman who taught her that she should sing from the heart and "what comes comes." Nancy was only in her early twenties but up until now, had existed within the spinsterish limitations of post-war family-led society. All at once, new friends were able to nourish her love of music and introduce her to new experiences. Through the Warres, another set of new acquaintances opened up to her, and she was invited to concerts in private London houses, formal, elegant affairs, all "gold chairs and white kid gloves". Mrs Warre was herself a musician and singer, and encouraged Nancy to join professional and amateur choirs. She auditioned successfully for The Bach Choir. Ralph Vaughan Williams was the conductor and listened to her sing. *'I can see him now, looking over his spectacles as I finished the sight reading, "not a bad piece of composing" was his only comment. He taught me what music was about and was in every respect a great man.'* The more Nancy sang, the happier she felt. The joy music and singing brought her filled her with a sense of profound gratitude and she wrote: *'With the Bach Choir the peak moments were the Palm Sunday performance of the St Matthew Passion. When I later joined the Philharmonic, a more professional choir, I had two unforgettable experiences. The first singing the Brahms Requiem under Sir Thomas Beecham, he danced about the rostrum like an intoxicated faun, spurring us on to sing as we had never sung before. The second a performance of the B Minor Mass in the Queen's Hall. I never felt nearer to heaven than I did singing the Sanctus.'*

The European trip with the Spencer-Smiths was several weeks of cultural feasting. They attended concerts, operas and art galleries and were entertained by the eminent and erudite. They stayed in the famously luxurious Sacher Hotel in the centre of Vienna, amused by the cigar puffing owner, Madame Sacher. Nancy found herself dancing in a Prague nightclub with exiled White Russians, who had been jettisoned to Prague, Paris and other European cities, refugees of the Russian Revolution. She remembered being "whizzed and whirled" around the dance floor to Viennese waltzes in the arms of Austrian Prince Kinsky, Czech Prince Lobkovitz and most intriguingly of all, she believed, Rasputin's reputed assassin, Prince Felix Yusupov. The Russian prince was not only was famous for being the man who helped hatch and carry out the plot to kill Rasputin, but also enjoyed appearing in ballgowns and jewellery at parties in his youth. *'There were frequent lunch parties of an immensely formal nature. At first I found it terribly hard not to giggle, but gradually became fairly adept at making the requisite bows as the occasion required,'* recalled Nancy. She and Penelope toured Vienna, Prague and Dresden together, soaking up music wherever they went. *'We often went to the Redouten-saal, a beautiful, small, baroque theatre, part of the Hofburg Palace where they put on Rossini and Mozart operas. On one especially grand occasion we went to the State Opera to hear Rosenkavalier conducted by Richard Strauss with the famous opera singer, Lottie Lehmann singing.'* As she wrote, Nancy's confidence and sense of herself was rising.

But by the early 1920's, music for Nancy wasn't limited to her own personal development, happiness and entertainment, it began to take her in an unexpected direction and it was far from palaces, glamorous Russian aristocrats, Strauss and Sachertorte. It was grass roots, fundamental and far closer to home.

'I knew I could sing but discovered I had a gift for getting people to sing. I seemed to have a little bit in my fingers with conducting.' Through the Ugley Women's Choir, Nancy began to realise that ordinary women's voices could be harnessed in an entirely new way. Like her maternal grandmother, even unwittingly, it was a feminist direction to take. It all seemed quite benign at first: a group of local rural women in a village getting together and singing some simple songs. 'The Ugley Womens' Choir' was perhaps not the most inspiring name, indeed it did inspire amusement but it represented the start of amateur choral singing for women; a form of empowerment that was inclusive, pleasurable and critically, unthreatening. Anyone was welcome. Education, birth and money were not necessary. Nor was the ability to play a musical instrument. All that was needed was a woman, her vocal chords and the requirement to leave her home and meet outside her domestic setting. Nancy was at the start and the centre of it.

Folk music and rural life are inseparable. In the same way that the

Women's Institute sought to preserve female-orientated rural skills and traditions (whether craft or cooking) through a community of women outside the home, the link between female rural identity and the celebration of the ordinary, by elevating it to a serious artistic endeavour, was quite radical. It wasn't surprising that folk music was a favourite genre. Music had hitherto been for men, rich people, religion and festivals. A secular, female group of singers was new.

Despite having no formal qualifications, Nancy could read music, had a good singing voice and played the piano well. She also had the time available to devote to any chosen occupation and thus it was that her ascent through the Women's Institute's hierarchy began to gather momentum. '*Step by step I got onto the Music Committee in the counties. I suppose they heard what I was up to, then we started arranging different competitions, community singing, that kind of thing.*' The Women's Institute was no stranger to music before Nancy became involved. From the very beginning, in Lorna Gibson's analysis, *Beyond Jerusalem: Music in the Women's Institute, 1919-1969,* the sort of music and songs that the network of WI choirs sang was centralised and the purpose of them was to be inclusive and easy to perform.

By 1923, William Blake's poem, *Jerusalem* was proposed as the Institute's song, '*Both words and music are simple and dignified and are easy to learn. Incidentally, the learning would give pleasure to any WI and would afford an excellent opportunity for a short talk either on Blake's poetry, or on poems about England.*' wrote Grace Haddow, the first Vice-Chairman of the WI in 1923. *Jerusalem* was undoubtedly associated with patriotism but the music was rooted in female emancipation. Hubert Parry's score was first sung collectively by suffragists at their meeting in the Royal Albert Hall in 1917. The meaning of the hymn (which has always been ruminated on but never entirely clear) was poignant. At a time when most women couldn't vote, talk of empowerment, action and endeavour seemed to be the stuff of Boudiccan determination.

Nancy would later write of *Jerusalem*, '*The first verse has as its theme the legend that Christ came to Britain as a child, but it really throws out a challenge. Blake is asking us what we think about our country, what does it mean to us with all its beauty and traditions? Do the right spiritual and physical conditions prevail in it for its people to develop what is best in themselves? In the second verse he answers the challenge and as we sing it we answer it too, for it is a challenge to the individual.'* The emancipation message was for women to look inward and consider themselves, and what they could offer, rather than what was traditionally expected of them.

On 9th July 1923 the first meeting of the National Federation Music Sub-Committee took place. One of the first decisions was to teach women how to conduct. Again, this was quietly subversive. Men were conductors. They commanded armies, fleets and orchestras. Even a century later, female conductors are vastly outnumbered by their male counterparts. In 1928, The Representation of the People Act was passed and all women over the age of 21 were allowed to vote. All women, regardless of their marital, social or financial status counted. They had finally found political expression. Nancy was busy finding their collective voices too and made sure they would be heard. The Women's Institute now began to refer to itself as the National Federation of Women's Institutes, or the NFWI, and began to mobilise choirs nationally. Nancy travelled relentlessly around the country, judging singing competitions, staying in wildly diverse accommodation. She loved it. One night she found herself at Chatsworth, soaking up the grandeur and hospitality of the Duchess of Devonshire, another night she was warmly received into 'a humble miner's cottage'. Her unsnobbish, practical Scottish background was serving her well, and her fellow Institute members benefited. Nancy's devotion to the power of music to bring women together became a lifelong conviction. By the 1930's, she had established choral singing competitions with thousands of Institute members.

'The adjudicator, Miss Nancy Tennant, congratulated the choirs on several occasions for their courageous singing of difficult songs. She repeated

her suggestion of last year that it was the significance of words and not changed tempo which conveys the feeling of a song . . .' reported the Monmouthshire Federation of Women's Institutes after a singing competition of fifteen WI choirs and two mixed choirs in 1936. *'Miss Tennant conducted all the choirs in massed singing of The Grasmers Carol by Somerville, and Thanksgiving by Dyson, a moving experience for every choir member.'*

CHAPTER SEVEN

The Latecomer

1919

'Peace meant Hagley but it also alas it meant school, in tears he was hurried off to England in scratchy tweed, replacing the sailor suits of home.'

The Great War was over and it was finally possible for the Waterfields to gain safe passage through France and across the Channel to England. It also meant it was time for Humphrey to join the cradle of The Establishment: the boarding school educational system. Packed off reluctantly from the world he had known, away from his family and the comfort and rhythms of the South of France, it was a question of survival of the fittest.

For all boarders, the end of the holidays would be marked by packing the hefty school trunk and tuck box, a ritual which generally provoked extreme gloom, not the thumping cheer of a girls' boarding school novel. Once strapped, the trunk would be 'sent ahead.' On the first day of term, parents with their uniformed sons descended on the capital, appearing in various grand hotels to consume a vast, final meal as a treat before dispersing to the relevant railway station for their respective trains. "I remember ordering grouse before going back to school, much to my father's fury," recalled once prep school veteran, as he and his brothers devoured their last lunch at the colossal Great Western Hotel before returning back to prep school. "Our greatest thrill was the hors d'oeuvre trolley which, for boys reared on a plain, nursery food diet, was inconceivably exotic. The very idea of being able to choose your own food rather than simply eating what you were given, and from a generous selection of exotic seafoods, cold meats and even pickles, was unbelievably exciting."

When they found the appointed platform, a very particular sight awaited. Well-dressed, smartly groomed groups of children and parents assembled on the platform, some cheerful and talkative, others stifling silent tears. One last embrace with their mothers; a firm handshake from their fathers, determined that neither they nor their offspring would betray any emotional weakness, and it was time to leave. The boys would find their appointed carriage, scramble aboard, the whistle would sound and their other, more familiar reality would begin. The separation periods were long and most children wouldn't see their parents and siblings again for months at a time.

The compulsion of the British upper classes to do as they had been done by as far as childhood was concerned found its most stark expression in their effective abandonment of extremely young boys. Lucky if you were in a pack of brothers, a natural protection unit, to warn a newcomer of predatory masters and unkind regimes, not so lucky if you were an eldest son, the first of your family to arrive at a large Victorian country house on a damp September afternoon. Cold knees, laced shoes, thick tweed and dormitories of rows of uncomfortable beds were standard. The food was famously basic. 'Dead Man's Shoulder', a lardy suet and boiled mince confection of savoury stodge as a main course would have been received with delight: it would at least fill a hungry and growing boy's stomach, improbable as this sounds today. Equally thrilling was the possibility of treacle sponge. Properly ripe tomatoes, olives or even the sweet buttery scent of a French boulangerie would have felt to Humphrey the stuff of a culinary dream. Corporal punishment was meted out on a daily basis, and codes of loyalty between boys were tight. Emotional displays were derided, crying was 'blubbing' and if caned by a master, however painful and humiliating the experience, the default reaction was to emerge from the room of admonishment and swagger back to fellow school friends, swanking about the quantity and severity of strokes that had been administered.

But this was not entirely Humphrey's experience. He didn't go to boarding school until he was ten. He spent what would have been the earliest prep school years at home instead, with his younger brother, Tony, and the beloved Betty Duff, his governess. *'It was impossible to think of the family at the Clos without thinking of Betty Duff. Tall, upright, Scottish to the backbone, she came as a young woman to be governess to the boys. She became the scaffolding of their family life. Between the wars, as Barbara's health deteriorated, Derick, despite his deep affection, his reading aloud, his care for Barbara, despite his piano playing and his tennis, became more detached and the household management (though Barbara always took charge of the menus) devolved on Betty or Babu as she was known. But this was done with such tact, such unselfish devotion that a casual observer might not have realised how much of the exquisitely run house owed to her,'* wrote Nancy.

In *'The Making of Them: The British Attitude to Children and The Boarding School System'* psychologist Nick Duffield argues the profound damage done to young children separated too early from their parents colours their adult relationships for life. Roald Dahl illustrated the emotional tangle well in his autobiographical book on childhood, entitled 'Boy': *'Unless you have been to a boarding school when you are very young, it is absolutely impossible to appreciate the delights of living at home. It is almost worth going away because it's so lovely coming back. I could hardly believe that I didn't have to wash in cold water in the mornings or keep silent in the corridors, or say 'Sir' to every grown-up man I met, or get flicked with wet towels while naked in the changing room, or eat porridge for breakfast that seemed to be full of little round sheep's-droppings, or walk all day long in perpetual fear of the long yellow cane that lay on top of the corner-cupboard in the Headmaster's study.'*

Ironically it was the First World War that saved Humphrey from such an early wrench away from home so that when he arrived at Temple Grove Preparatory school, he was an older, less malleable, less vulnerable child. It was too late to be institutionalized. He may have been apprehensive, but now, by the age of ten, he had developed a mind of his own and had the confidence to express his own opinions. He and his father travelled to England together, leaving his mother in France with his brother. In time-honoured fashion, he was deposited at the appointed time and place in a London railway station with droves of other boys, said his last farewell and boarded the train. His cousin Duncan Gardner wrote: *'I can well remember the scene on the platform . . . when I was being sent off for the first time in the charge of [my] brother Selby who was in his third year at the school. This did not prevent him from weeping bitterly, while I stood by pale and shivering with misery. Nine years in a lovely warm home, an adoring mother and friendly, respectful governess and servants – then, suddenly, a cold, unknown great world, with no expectation of any human warmth, indeed a certainty of chilly indifference, if nothing worse. And the reality proved as bad as the dread; so that in later life I vowed I would not send my children away so young. Nevertheless it should always be remembered that it is almost impossible for a normal child to be miserable all the time; and indeed I couldn't have been, for I can remember several things I liked – such as fooling around with friendly boys, cricket, football and sugar biscuits in bed . . .'*

Humphrey's arrival at Temple Grove typified his approach throughout his life. The accomplished polymath he would eventually become might have been regarded as an absent-minded liability. *'His arrival there was characteristic. Getting out of the train he followed what he thought were the nicest boys, only to discover he was in the wrong school. The mistake discovered, a reluctant Waterfield was removed to his appointed destination. All his life he was detached from practicalities'*, recorded Nancy. It wasn't an institution entirely alien and unloving. The headmaster was his cousin.

Temple Grove Preparatory School at the time was situated in a large mansion in Eastbourne. In the 19th century, under the legendary hand of a relation, Ottiwell Waterfield, it had become an establishment of choice for the English aristocracy and landed gentry. By the time Humphrey arrived, the baton had passed to another Waterfield relation, The Reverend H W Waterfield who was well-liked. Typical of prep schools of the era, it was a large country house with extensive grounds. A few games pitches would have been created from the surrounding acres but they would have borne no relation to the semi-professional sports grounds of glossy private prep schools a century later. This particular establishment, a Victorian Gothic redbrick, was run along rigorous lines. The main privations for the pupils would have been cold, hunger and the humiliation of corporal punishment. It was so cold at night that ice formed on the boys' bed clothes.

Prep and public schools function best for the pupil experiencing them when everyone buys into the same culture. Humphrey was beyond it both emotionally and geographically. He simply hadn't been through the system in the same way as other boys had. He was chaotic yet bright and intellectually inquisitive when he wanted to be. *'I arrived, a queer, foreign-spoken exhibit at my prep-school, [expected] to make what terms I could with the home-bred product,'* he recalled.

Aged 13 he moved on to public school and was sent to Eton, like the other men in his family. Just as his arrival had been at Temple Grove, his start was cheerfully muddled. Again, he found himself in the wrong building. This time, he went to the wrong boarding house. A confusing moment, soon resolved. He made friends easily. *'Humphrey Waterfield first came into my life in 1922,'* wrote Cas Jones-Mortimer, his life-long school friend, *'and he remained one of my best and oldest friends. He was well-liked by everybody and friendly to all, going out of his way to be kind to non-starters and freaks of all types. Neither of us was much good at rowing or any form of athletics. He played football and Fives with some zest and inaccuracy. The only game at which he was better than most of us was tennis. This we used to laugh off by saying it was because he lived in France. But when it came to schoolwork he was better than most of us and started learning subjects for fun long before we others learnt them for anything more than necessity. In my mind's eye I can see him now, seated at his burry, an Eton word believed to be a corruption of the inacceptable and foreign, 'bureau', assiduously reading Dante from cover to cover. This he achieved with the aid of an Italian grammar and dictionary, together with the learned notes of some dead scholar with whose name we were unac- quainted. He often gave me the impression of reading about four books at one and the same time. When thus employed he did not welcome interruption by us for more frivolous and useless pursuits of a non- academic nature such as football and the like. We went together to the annual OTC camps. He wasn't good at being a boy soldier and I was little better.'*

The separation from home and family life in France was mollified by his very real delight in staying at Hagley in short holidays when Humphrey journeyed up to his mother's childhood home in Staffordshire to stay with his beloved Great Aunt Meta. It made for an emotionally complicated but independent minded child. From a young age he thought for himself and regarded himself as something slightly beyond the conventional boundaries. Years later, during the Second World War, when Humphrey was stationed in Tobruk in 1941, he wrote, 'The Trees', a short story about a small five-year old boy called John rejoicing in the beauty of his surroundings: *'It had been a wonderful walk over the park. The hedges were a little thin on top, the year's nests jumped to the eye lightly veiled by Traveller's Joy in all its smoky beauty. The lovely leaves of yellowing willow pointed the streaked clarity of autumn sky. Mushrooms, too, lit up the sulky green of the meadows, microcosmically reflecting with their tiny cupolas and tarnished pewter surfaces.'*

The rhythm of Christmas and Easter spent at Le Clos and half terms and summer holidays at Hagley ended abruptly. In the early 1920's, when he was still at Eton, his Great Aunt Meta became ill and moved out of Hagley. In 1924, the estate was sold and little by little, the house was demolished. Meta died in 1926. In 1940, an embittered and nostalgic Humphrey wrote: *'Hagley lay a year or two in the market but found no takers. The town had not the courage or the money to buy if for a civic centre: it was squalidly sold to a speculator who stripped it of its Adam decorations and more than repaid himself for his pains. Its beauty was frittered away by a generation no longer able or desirous of upholding the older ways of life, not bold nor imaginative enough to construct a better way for the future. Private beauty yielded not to public beauty, but to public ugliness; the dream of an aristocrat to the vulgar greed of the speculator.'* This wrench would inform his sense of loss for the rest of his life. *'My paradise is lost and can never be regained!'* he wailed in his journal, when revisiting the pain of the destruction of his English eden. *'And so a flower, a tree, a particular woodland, a picture, a piece of furniture, even a look in the sky, all have power to torment me, to whip me to a passionate, fruitless longing for their counterpart at some earlier, happier time.'*

CHAPTER EIGHT

Romance and Rebellion

Oxford 1927

'To be sensitive and to have an intellect, is probably the greatest misfortune that man may have. It is like thundering blindfold in the dark, and coming continuously up against hard walls. At every moment one knocks into the selfishness, the vested interest, the stupidity of all the innumerable congregations of mankind.'

B y September 1927, Humphrey was fully fledged. Tall, with thick dark hair and warm brown eyes, he was good looking, charming, tri-lingual and opinionated. The tearful boy who had been shuttled off to England for his education had become a quirky young Oxford undergraduate. Spiritually he felt he belonged to both the lost paradise of his aunt's house in Staffordshire and the dry heat of his parents' Mediterranean idyll. In his diary Humphrey wrote, on his arrival at Christ Church College:'. . . *how cold it seemed and grey, but what lightness, what keenness in the air! And the gentle rain brushing against the windowpane, so different from the steady Mediterranean downpour, and the clouds, and the sun breaking through the clouds, and joining with rainbows, the poplars on either side of the river . . . grass, real grass, perennial not needing to be sown each year. It was a miracle!'*

Humphrey had left Eton in 1926. It is likely he spent Christmas in Menton with his family, but the following spring he set off for a transatlantic adventure, on what would now be thought of as a gap year, before going up to Oxford. On the 21st March he embarked on the Providence Passenger Ship at Nice. He was not alone. Accompanied by two Menton families, Thomas and Joan Kenny and Canadian born Edward Knox Leet, his wife Mary and their two children, the the youngest of whom was three and it promised to be a convivial and jolly trip. He arrived at Rhode Island on the 9th May and made his way north to the vast beauty of Ontario to stay with Waterfield cousins. His widowed aunt, Mabel Snooks, was there to receive him at her ranch house where he was to help with the cattle. He loved the vast space and raw natural beauty of the Canadian landscape, enjoying the strenuous, outdoor ranch life. The peace and enormity of the lakes left a lasting impression.

During his first few weeks at university, Humphrey felt like a small glittering minnow swimming into the jaws of a whale. He wondered whether he might be swallowed whole by the intellectual influences and stimulation of Oxford and dreaded losing his independence of mind. He was already battling internally against an upbringing steeped in traditional expectation and emotional repression. Superficially he knew he could toe the conventional line, slipping seamlessly from one familiar territory to another. Filtered through Eton's gaze, itself modelled on an Oxbridge system with its collegiate structure, large chapel and other ancient buildings, arriving at Oxford, another all-male institution, was easy. Although female students were now admitted, they were few and strictly segregated in their own colleges. Only from the year of Humphrey's arrival were they allowed to sit the same examinations as men. Prior to that, women were limited to the 'freedom' of academic study without presenting their failures or successes for scrutiny in a public arena. When they were finally allowed to pursue an identical education to men, their numbers were controlled.

Humphrey chose to read History at Christ Church, the grandest and most imposing of all the Oxford colleges. Founded in the sixteenth century, the honey-coloured collection of buildings boasted their own cathedral, an enormous bell tower and vast quads. The college attracted similarly aristocratic undergraduates. Counting more prime ministers amongst its alumni than any other university college in the world, it was a place where political and diplomatic skills were honed to perfection, as previous Waterfield generations had discovered. Humphrey didn't care. Convention stifled him, not least because he didn't really need to exist in one single place. With his sense of belonging or 'home' split between Britain and Europe, he didn't really 'come from' anywhere in particular, which freed him from feeling an obligation to the Establishment and its expectations. *'He was happy there, but rather an odd man out. His friends were mostly from richer and more sporting backgrounds, he took little part in college activities and affected particularly to despise those who rode horses and fired guns,'* according to his friend Cas Mortimer.

As well as throwing himself into his subject, Humphrey was awash with adolescent sentiments and the raw passions of youth. Nature, its beauty and power lay at the heart of all his emotion. Its transient quality became a conduit for lost paradise and happiness (no doubt Hagley and even more deeply a sense of his mother's grief over the loss of baby Sylvia), absence and joy. Withering trumpets of late summer honeysuckle triggered a mournful outpouring of lost pleasures and the fragility of the natural world, *'today, walking in the lanes . . . I saw what I am terribly afraid will be the last honeysuckle of the year. Living habitually in towns, we allow the seasons to slip imperceptibly from us; travelling 'abroad' we run through them backwards very often, like as at a cinema, and get long reels of them repeated. But in the country, and in one place, it is different and with a pang I realise that I shall never again taste this year, the sweet poignant scent of the honeysuckle hanging on the evening hedges. I love winter with its mystery, and autumn with its intangible pomp and colours; but who will give me back the honey pale myrtle flowers that ever since I first buried myself among, as a small boy in Cornwall, I have ever mystically adored?'*

Like a Romantic disciple of Shelley or Keats, his sense of the power of nature and beauty sometimes overwhelmed him. There is almost a hint of the manic: '*Quite by chance I found myself out of doors at ten o'clock. . . . I have never faced such a night as this. The absolute loneliness of the Downs, the sullen immobile shapes of the dark clumps of trees; the strange sweep of the boughs of solitary wind tossed trees, that appalling moon . . . brought one suddenly face to face with a pagan reality there was nothing in this stark, open world, nothing at all: all was vanity; the fields of corn that bowed and swirled invincible in the darkness, acknowledged it. Man was nothing; a light thing; and all the changes beneath the moon were impotent beside the eternal verity of this implacable sky.*'

The university college gardens were also places of beauty and wonder. As his friend Cas also recalled, 'Humphrey's rooms at the House were in Tom Quad on the ground floor of the south side of the entrance to the cathedral. I think Humphrey's interest and delight in the creation of gardens sprang from about this time of his life. Unlike many an Oxford college, the House possessed no garden, but during Humphrey's time there a garden of a sort was devised on the east side of the college. In the construction of this he showed great interest. A portion of the old city wall on which some ancient fig-trees grew, formed the northern boundary. There was but one other tree, a sycamore, just inside the entrance to the garden. This, Humphrey seized upon as an object of great beauty and I remember teasing him by telling him that it was useless as timber, a consideration that naturally passed him by. We were however united in our admiration of the magnificent oriental plane tree visible from the college garden against the cathedral."

As well as developing his profound love of the natural world and its importance to him, his views on British society had begun to crystallize. There were plenty of people at Oxford and in the country who thought the same as him. He may have rubbed along with the variously traditional or flamboyant, upper-class undergraduates around him, but he didn't consider himself one of them or try to ingratiate himself into their circles. He was an outsider and enjoyed being one.

His views on society began to express themselves in his semi-autobiograpical essay, *The Trees*, which was written in his thirties: '*John woke up one morning, looked back at his life, and decided the best of his years were over. He was always doing the wrong thing: holding his hand to strangers as he had been taught, and blushing hot when it was ignored. Life was full of these gaffes which ate into the heart like acid and could never be expunged.*'

Humphrey regarded British social structure with irritation and began to kick back against his background. He was no serious revolutionary, but he enjoyed questioning the merit of a system based on land ownership insofar as it prevented him or anyone else walking wherever they wanted through the landscape. Nor did he approve of the killing of game for sport: '*There is no doubt that shooting is no more cruel than hunting . . . My objection I think is due to the enormous amount of selfishness which shooting entails . . . It is the business of artificially preserving enormous quantities of open country almost continuously that is so annoying. Personally, I resent being excluded from the loveliest downs and hilltops in the interest of what is after all the selfish desire of a few people to indulge their atavistic drive for killing . . .*' In 1927, in a precursor to the infamous King and Country Oxford Union debate of 1933, the Cambridge Union voted against armed combat, "*That lasting peace can only be secured by the people of England adopting an uncompromising attitude of pacifism*". The motion was passed and hardly caused a ripple beyond the Cambridge undergraduates, but the seeds of pacifism were germinating everywhere. Nonagression appealed to Humphrey. Friends remembered him walking the streets of Oxford wearing placards advocating pacifism. Following the First

World War, the dread of another pointless decimation of an entire generation infused the collective consciousness.

Like the 1960s *Love and Peace* movement forty years later, the youthful backlash to the wrongs of the previous ruling class was not a small fringe movement. Pacifism and Pacificism weren't simply anti-war sentiments, they were expressions of collective exasperation. Prior to the First World War, rulers ruled and the masses generally did what they were told. No longer. Bolsheviks had triumphed in Russia and the concept of mass protest forcing new social order and value systems had caught hold. Slogans *"Never Again"* and *"No More War"* represented more than a public sentiment. It was a shift in collective opinion. And like the 21st century Brexit movement, it was a simmering threat to the status quo.

Humphrey knew he didn't want to be the next generation of diplomatic Waterfield stewards of the Empire. He was different. His father, despite his own father's illustrious diplomatic career in the Raj, was not unsympathetic. Derick and Humphrey reached an agreement, if Humphrey could get a First Class Degree, he would be allowed to go to Art School. The Ruskin School of Drawing in Oxford was the obvious first place. Foreign Office exams and a diplomatic career would have to wait.

Humphrey also knew he was no workaholic. Much as he loved the intellectual pursuit of academia, it was the raw beauty of nature and his desire to paint that overwhelmed him. His notebooks were partly filled with profound academic ponderings, but they were also bursting with his own thoughts and sketches on life, love, women, men and beauty. Some of his poetic scrawlings were fairly terrible but they reveal his romantic sensibilities and preoccupations:

Tomorrow, she comes tomorrow
Shout out my heart with glee
Where with foam curled and tempest hurled
Ships awaits the sea

Oh gentle winds, release her
Receive her lightly, star
For oh these nests, between her breasts that
All that is life to me.

Etc etc.

But striding around the countryside in his spare time like an "eighteenth century figure" pronouncing on landownership, God, Beauty and the passing seasons wasn't necessarily time well spent. A more rigorous character would have eschewed the distracting Romantic urges and settled down to serious academic study. But Humphrey despised work for its own sake. He wanted illumination not accolades: *'there is something divine indeed in a man who can see all created things in a light in which nothing is too small or unimportant. And with the joy of the artist in understanding, and the infinite power to enjoy. The curse of modern civilization is the economic pressure which forces the bodies of men into incessant and insufficiently rewarded toil, and their minds into a restless vacinity (sic). Earthly kings & empires perish, but who shall say when the imperial insect has its end? That is the true use of books, to enlarge one's emotional experience. Books read for the accumulation of knowledge, unless knowledge is directed to some such end, represent in this view good time wasted.'*

He sat his Finals in the summer of 1930. He had gambled. He had undoubtedly whiled away countless hours and even days indulging his sensibilities. He loved History, but he loved art and the world around him more. His quality of degree would either signal liberation into Creativity, Beauty and Truth or what he regarded as mindless 'toil'. His papers were duly marked and the History dons discussed their merits or lack of them. A few weeks later, on a wet summer's morning, Humphrey made his way down Oxford's High Street, and headed for The Examination Schools. It was time to face the music and his future as an adult. It was results day.

CHAPTER NINE

Man and Artist

1930

'So paltry a thing as a First Class in the History Schools'

Humphrey parked his car as close as he could to the Examination Schools and slammed the door shut. He turned off the High Street and entered the imposing Victorian building. Having to seek out results by foot, along with numerous other nervous candidates, all staring at the lists in a building inspired by a seventeenth century manor house, was enough to set most people's teeth on edge. For Humphrey it was a life-defining moment. Everything depended on this. He walked towards the results boards, thinking that he really should have managed it; after all, in his second year at Oxford he had been awarded an unsolicited scholarship. Confident now that he knew he was clever enough, as he scanned the names at the top of the list where the Firsts should be, his name was missing. There wasn't anything in the Second-Class degrees either. Or the Thirds. Not only was his name nowhere to be seen, but none of his friends seemed listed either. Humid summer rain began to fall. It was a proper disaster.

Crushed, Humphrey now knew there would be no Ruskin, no subsequent legitimacy as an artist. He would just have to fit in and plod along the well-trodden Waterfield imperialist path. Others crammed around him, scanning for their names and degree results, all sharing the expectation, the panic, elation or disappointment. But before he descended into a genuine spiral of despair, Humphrey realised he was looking at the wrong names. He had been staring at the women's results. Just like the ten-year old prep schoolboy on the train ending up at the wrong school; the older boy at Eton arriving at the wrong house, he had rushed towards something without paying attention. His eyes flicked up the men's list. He was at the very top. He had scored the highest First in his year: '. . . so, before I had even a moment's pang, a little higher up there it was . . . and then rushing to the car I set off, singing and yelling poetry through the rain, and swerving and skidding and happy . . .'

As Humphrey drove out of Oxford, leaving his three undergraduate years behind him, he felt increasingly ecstatic. Soon the city gave way to fields as he motored south towards the Downs: 'The sky was the brightest blue, and the foreground of sun and the golden stretches of corn, and in among the corn innumerable bright black speckles as the rooks gorged themselves upon it. And I was extremely happy, for had I not proved that it was possible to care chiefly for corn and the rooks among it, and yet to equal the scholars at their own game? "Art is Joy"; and Joy is Art together had broken through bonds of solemn learning, where they did not properly belong; so that I felt like Sassoon; captive, escaping, bird 'winging wildly across the white orchards & dark green.' And the world seemed one endless vista of intense blue sky and of golden gleaming corn; so that there is something to be said – so vain are we for achieving even so paltry a thing as a First Class in the History Schools . . .'

For some, the accolade and satisfaction would have fuelled a desire for further academic immersion. Following his First, he was invited to sit the exams for All Souls College, the post graduate Oxford college for the brightest stars of any graduate year. He decided against it. He was determined to follow his heart. It had to be Art School and the life of an artist next.

In 1930, the Ruskin School of Drawing was in the Ashmolean Museum, a moment's walk from his old college. Ruskin's approach to art, nature, life and human happiness were the same as Humphrey's. *'Fine art is that in which the hand, the head and the heart of man go together'* John Ruskin had declared, not simply as an aesthetic but as a social and political movement. Not only did it chime with the values Humphrey had formed as an undergraduate, but the prospect of living a more bohemian life of spontaneity was irresistible. Like a dormant butterfly released from the cocoon of his Establishment education, Humphrey began to realise that the world could be both thrilling and authentic. Ruskin, the social revolutionary and master teacher of drawing may have died before Humphrey born, but his legacy was rock solid. Ruskin's collection of Old Masters, including drawings, paintings and prints from Turner to Dürer, provided the art students with direct inspiration for their drawing classes. Ruskin had been the *enfant terrible* of 19th century British art. Dispensing with what was known as the 'South Kensington' method of teaching (essentially a strict and technical approach to drawing), with pains-taking incremental steps to accomplishment, he believed in expressive learning rather than theoretical repetitive rigour.

Humphrey's tutor was Albert Rutherston, a member of the preco-ciously art-mad German Jewish Rothenstein family. Albert was a well-known painter and set designer in his own right, and his brothers were the celebrated portrait painter Sir William Rothenstein (Albert had anglicised his Jewish surname) and the art collector and busi-nessman, Charles Rutherston. A short, dark-haired pixie-faced man, Albert and his wife Marjory were to become close friends with Humphrey in the ensuing years - and ultimately shape his future.

The hand and head may have been working well together, but Humphrey's emotional development had been arrested by his moth-er's limited supply of love, preventing his progression into a living, breathing romance of his own. His diaries were filled with musings and amateur poems, still pretty purple with blatant borrowings from Shelley and Keats. He burst with passion and longing but was unable to project it onto a real person, let alone a real relationship. Instead, Nature, Beauty and abstract women were the objects of his ardour, tangled up in a romantic universe of loss and frustrated passion:

'When I wore the world on a golden ring
In other days with you
And bound up every lovely thing
In one thread of silver dew
And round my mind would twine and swing
Phylacteries of you'

His observations on nature and the landscape were much more effective, and studying at Ruskin allowed him to properly indulge his ideas. It could be said that these next years were formative in developing his later talent for garden landscape, form and design, just as much as for his art. When he wasn't wandering England's country footpaths communing with Nature, Humphrey travelled to France to visit his parents for the Christmas and Easter holidays. He filled his diaries with strong visual images of the places he visited. He rejoiced in the colour, form and beauty that surrounded him, whether man-made or natural. Whether in the empty Downs of southern England or the warm, richness of Mediterranean life in Menton, he consigned his thoughts to his diaries. The world before him was a visual, sensorial feast. Engagement with it was part of the process of being a true artist. *And then there is the market – a ridiculous 1911 building, all yellow, with garlands of turquoise and green and orange and lemon fruit and leaves to crown it. It is one of the tourist legends of eternal sunshine and metal blue oleographic seas in postcards . . . the lightly clad boys with splendid figures whose firm and delicate arms it is a pleasure even with the eye to draw and the old chattering women, stooping over baskets of fruit and vegetables.'* His love of nature was a transcendental passion, overwhelming any earthly stirrings or desires. And it wasn't just the approach to art. His social circle altered. He began to define himself far beyond the patrician limitations of an Eton education and Oxford degree. He was now friends with artists and fellow creative thinkers.

After a year he progressed on to The Slade School of Fine Art in London, and a life based in Bloomsbury. He loved it. Living on a pittance, he joined The London Group: a self-selected group of artists who objected to the Royal Academy's 'stranglehold' on exhibiting radical new work. Formed from the former Campden Town Group and the English Cubists in 1918, by the time Humphrey joined it, the group's output was diverse and counted Bloomsburyites Roger Fry, Clive and Vanessa Bell and Duncan Grant amongst its members.

His weekends were often spent with his cousins Duncan and Violet Gardner. One such weekend in 1933, he found himself in animated conversation with a fellow pacifist, Margaret Birley, Nancy Tennant's sister. Forty-year-old Margaret, now Mrs Birley, was still beautiful and bristling with energy. After the initial misery of her early widowhood in 1914 during the First World War, she met and married Dr Jim Birley, a neurologist, in 1922. She was now a mother of four: her eldest, Ariel, was already a young woman and there were three more children. Margaret took an instant shine to Humphrey. He was young, just twenty-four, clearly brilliantly intelligent and talented. He shared her views on The Peace Ballot and pacifism. She also thought he would be a perfect addition to Ariel's social circle; Ariel, who also loved art and had ambitions to paint. She invited him to her daughter's 19th birthday weekend. The Ugley family in the Ugley village, which of course sounded hilarious. What fun. Humphrey liked Margaret, said he would love to come and would arrive by train.

CHAPTER TEN

Fascist Friends

1932

"Thank you miss, but I don't hold with maps."

Nancy was doing more than her music committee work. She also wanted to promote peace between former enemies. An international network of women was the perfect way to start. In the early 1930's she had become Chairman of the International Committee for the WI. Her ambition was simple: *'We had to try to think of people as people. I was particularly keen on the international side because when the WI started, they [the members] had no clue about other countries or that other people were like themselves. They were just sorry for others because they weren't English. I remember trying to show a woman a map of the Middle East where her son had gone and she said, "thank you miss, but I don't hold with maps."'*

~

Nancy wasn't the only member of her family trying to forge the bonds of friendship and mutual understanding between former enemy nations. Like his sisters, Ernest Tennant had been horrified by the losses of the Great War and by the mid-1930s, the young artist who painted the picture of his little sister standing in a garden at the turn of the century, had become influential in Anglo-German relations. Nancy's surviving brother was a natural leader. Dark haired, good-looking, with a saturnine, penetrating gaze, he was not short on confidence and the courage of his convictions. He cut a dominating figure and was as comfortable in international circles as he was on the hunting field. Married to Noni, a beautiful, volatile Italian, his four children would become the next generation of Orford Tennants. Following in his father's footsteps, Ernest joined the London branch of the family business, C Tennant Sons & Co Ltd. at 9 Mincing Lane in the heart of the City. Like his father, he was the financial brain behind the accumulation of the Tennant fortune (ensuring that future Tennants like Colin Glenconner could spend it at will). In 1894, Ernest's cousin Margot Tennant had married the Liberal Prime Minister HH Asquith, cementing the Tennant family's sense of duty and responsibility, which Ernest felt flowed through his veins as naturally as his Scottish, Liberal blood. He had travelled widely throughout his adult life and was fluent in German.

~

Today, Ernest's legacy divides historians. Some regard him as a stooge of Nazi Germany: a Hitler appeaser and friend of the gloriously handsome, vain and ultimately damned Joachim von Ribbentrop. Old Etonian and butterfly-collector, von Ribbentrop, who would later become German Ambassador to Great Britain in 1936, had tried to promote confidence in Nazi Germany through the work of The Anglo-German Fellowship. Those who knew Ernest better remember a serious character, who, like his two sisters, was determined that the horrors of the First World War which had expunged their generation, their cousins and most painfully their precious brother and brother-in-law, should never be repeated. Nor should Germany fall to the power of the Communists. Ernest was prepared to risk everything to achieve it.

~

Nancy, in later years, described Ernest as 'misguided'. His naïve, schoolboy belief in a select group of public-school alumni, with their upper lips stiffened against the increasingly awful realities of 1930s Germany, would ultimately cost him his reputation. In 1933, Ernest gave a lecture at Ashridge College, explaining his impression of the positive transformation that had taken place in Germany since 1919. He described the wretched state the country had been in after the end of the First World War which he had experienced first-hand. 'I was sent by the War Office on the first mission to Berlin after the Armistice – that was in January 1919. There was not a dog or cat to be seen – all had been eaten and their skin used for leather . . . there was no soap – even at the Adlon Hotel, the Ritz of Berlin, we had cakes of baked clay and sand . . . I am assured that during a period of two years in 1918-1919, over fifty per cent of women in childbirth died from lack of nourishment . . . Unless the blockade is raised at an early date there would seem to be grave danger of Germany going Bolshevik . . .". Ernest further explained to his audience that a new generation of Germans was emerging into adulthood which had only known extreme poverty, starvation and a country verging on Bolshevik revolution. As an alternative to Bolshevism, the new leader of the National Socialist Party not only delivered hope and purpose, he also implemented practical economic solutions. The Treaty of Versailles had damaged and humiliated Germany with post-war reparations and sanctions, and therefore Germany didn't want anyone it perceived as an outsider controlling it again. The Germans turned inwards and began to rebuild their country, re-inventing a national identity that bore no real relation to jigsaw of quite distinct Germanic kingdoms that had preceded it.

~

Backing up Ernest's appeal in 1933, it did appear as if the new Germany was gaining momentum. After raging inflation and a succession of short-lived ineffectual governments, the country was transformed. Industry was thriving and there was plenty of food. The *Hitlerjugend* and the *Bund Deutscher Mädel* had enrolled thousands of teenagers who spent their time in hearty, outdoor pursuits. With its rich history of art, music and culture the country was now a wholesome place to study, take a bracing holiday or sightsee. *'Everywhere in this country of infinite variety, the most hospitable of welcomes awaits you. Throughout Germany – in mountain villages, in mediaeval towns, in the depths of the mighty forests or beside the banks of the romantic Rhine – you will meet the friendly hospitality for which she is renowned'* declared Thomas Cook in a 1934 travel advertisement.

~

This was in total contrast with Britain, plunged into depression after the Wall Street crash of 1929, now suffering associated unemployment, bad food and terrible weather. Well-to-do English families saw no harm in resuming the traditional practice of sending their daughters to 'finish' what their French and German governesses had begun, and so one by one English girls began to return to the Continent. In 1933, after studying in France and honing her French, it was time for Ariel to go to art school in Munich and improve her German. Nancy would go as her companion and chaperone for the intial days and together they would meet Ariel's Munich landlady. It promised to be fun. Nancy had enjoyed plenty of German hospitality in the late 1920s and spoke the language a little. After visiting the reassuringly Hansel and Gretel prettiness of Munich, a visit to Berlin was on the itinerary and they stayed with Nancy's friends, the Berthouds. There was also another

Berlin resident on their list of contacts, who was more than delighted to extend an invitation. Ernest had made a new and charming friend.

~

Joachim von Ribbentrop was an undeniably attractive man. Looking more like a clean-cut, preppy American, he was fluent in French and English, musical and a patron of artists. He had travelled widely, having worked in Canada and the United States, returning to Europe as a travelling wine importer. In the early 1930's at least, he appeared to Ernest to be a kindred spirit, being as cosmopolitan as he. Ribbentrop had many Jewish friends, several of them artists. It must have been hard to see past his charm and apparent similarity. He, like Ernest, was openly vocal in his horror of Bolshevism and the danger it posed to Germany and beyond.

Ribbentrop was the archetypal social climber born into a middle-class, military family. Desperate to ingratiate himself with powerful circles at home and abroad, it was adoption by his aunt, Gertrud von Ribbentrop, which allowed him to add the crucial 'von' to his surname, conferring the aristocratic status required to breach the outer walls of European nobility. Ribbentrop was already close to leading Nazis and regarded by Hitler as the perfect smooth-talking 'salesman' to represent the emerging new Germany abroad. Indeed, many of his less successful but socially superior colleagues disparagingly referred to him as 'the wine merchant' even after Hitler appointed him British Ambassador in 1936. Schmoozing the 1930's London party scene, from grand dinners to private members' clubs and country house parties, the fair-haired Adonis charmed everyone, including Nancy. Following a visit to Orford House, she invited him to tea at the House of Commons with her friend, Patrick Buchan-Hepburn, who was Secretary to Winston Churchill, on the basis that he was "the nicest sort of German."

~

In Berlin it was inevitable that the Ribbentrops would invite Nancy to dinner. Against the advice of her hosts, Nancy accepted the invitation, looking forward to an interesting evening, deciding that she was old enough to make her own mind up. It certainly promised to be high profile as the former Prime Minister, David Lloyd George, would be attending. In the event, the party turned out to be awash with high profile Nazis; Hitler's Commander in Chief, General Blomberg; the ruthlessly ambitious Göring, famously thick-set and pompous, looking like a "gorilla in white satin with a bosom full of medals" and Ernst 'Putzi' Hanfstaengl, the part American, Harvard-educated, Munich art publisher, who also happened to be Hitler's Foreign Press Advisor. He was placed next to Nancy at dinner and flirtatiously asked her what she wanted to do in Berlin. Nancy suggested a glimpse of the Führer. She meant a fleeting glimpse, possibly as he drove past in a car. The opportunity to charm the sister and niece of pro-German Ernest Tennant was irresistible. The next morning, the Berthoud's telephone rang. Putzi, had arranged for both Nancy and Ariel to be taken to the Reichskanzlei, Hitler's Chancellery. Suddenly the two women were swept up in a sort of nightmare. "I was horrified. It was very wrong." said Nancy afterwards. A car arrived to collect them, and they hurtled towards Hitler's HQ.

～

The Reichskanzlei was imposing architecturally, and was swarming with Hitler's staff and troops. The atmosphere was military and severe – the hapless Tennant women were terrified. They were led down a "long corridor with goose-stepping soldiery" towards a room and told to wait outside. Nancy's primary thought was to "get out in one piece" as the attitude towards them felt as if arrest for some unknown crime was about to take place. The first to greet them was Rudolf Hess, who Nancy felt seemed more normal than the rest. She was told to remove her glasses, "as Hitler didn't like them." Eventually they were led into the room and the moustachioed Nazi leader presented himself. She felt a sinister, hypnotic, aura emanating from the Führer. His startling blue eyes rested on hers. He asked her what she thought of the "new Germany". Through her faltering German she replied that she it was very different from the former country. It seemed the only way to be polite enough to survive the meeting but hanging on a thread of principle, suggested things in the country she had known previously had altered.

They did get out in one piece, but Nancy never visited Germany again. The interview with Hitler had been chilling, yet it didn't stop Nancy and the International Committee believing that extending the hand of friendship would triumph over the aggressive iconography of Hitler's Germany: *'We tried to make people understand that nations were interdependent. We realised that a great moral and spiritual urge towards co-operation and good fellowship had arisen spontaneously among women in different parts of the world.'*

~

In the meantime, the excitements of Munich beckoned. As Rachel Johnson put it, speaking about her book *Winter Games,* "In Bavaria they had the crisp mountain air, a healthy life, the opera, the mountains and handsome Germans in uniform. They couldn't believe their luck! No chaperons, no parents. They had everything, including sex." By 1934, where her cousin the artist Derek Hill was studying costume and theatre design, Ariel had struck up an intriguing new friendship with Unity Mitford, who was also living in Munich and was famously smitten by all things Nazi. As Ariel recalled, *'When Diana [Guinness] and Unity first arrived in Munich, Derek and I were waiting on the platform to greet them. Diana came towards us with a beaming smile, "Darlings, what bliss! First time on a train, without Nanny or a husband!"'*

The Anglo-German Fellowship, founded by Lord Mount Temple, Ernest Tennant and Philip Conwell-Evans in 1935, was finally launched. The idea was to foster a close relationship between the economic and political movers and shakers of both countries. To Ernest's mind, the Fellowship would resemble an elite group of self-selected public-school prefects. The senior boys could sort things out for the rest of the 'school' – in other words, Europe. Tennant expressed his view of the proposed relationship between the emerging, thrusting young Nazi Germany and the wisdom and experience of Britain as follows:

> *'England is still mainly governed by an aristocracy with ancient traditions basically unchanged for centuries. Germany is governed by one comparatively young man risen from low beginning with no personal experience of other countries and surrounded by advisers of similar type . . . I still believe that it should not only be possible, but easy, to make friends with them. From 1933 to 1935 they looked upon Britain much as a new boy looks upon a house master . . .'*

Nancy's idea of a communion of peaceful women leading the way in mutual understanding may have appeared different on paper, but the motivation was like her brother's:

> *'I was concerned as Chairman of International Committee of the NFWI to try to get people to think in terms of Germans being like us struggling along in their villages, it was same for the French when France fell. To get away from this awful thing of hating the Germans from the First World War. It seemed to me we must have something to build on once the war was over. We had a lot of people coming to us to start it in other countries.'*

It is difficult for a modern reader to grasp how strong the public appetite for appeasement was in Britain at that point. Extending a metaphorical olive branch to what had previously been the enemy, or at least following a policy of nonaggression was a priority for most people. The Peace Ballot of 1934-35, the nationwide questionnaire in

Britain of five questions attempting to discover the British public's attitude to the League of Nations and armaments, proved this. In February 1934, Nancy packed her bags for Europe once again, but this time it was not for a cultural tour or high jinks with unsavoury characters. She headed to The International Congress in Brussels as the NFWI delegate and spoke for disarmament and lasting peace. But her passions that year would not only be political. 1934 was also the year she fell deeply and gloriously in love.

CHAPTER ELEVEN

The Ugley Family

1933

"Half a white waistcoat and an evening shoe."

Humphrey had already missed one train and knew he was likely to miss the next. He was leaving his Bloomsbury digs in a rush, as he always did. He needed to take formal evening dress - that was easy, as he already had it. But slow, orderly packing was not something that interested him. It was awful and dull. Why not look at the light on the trees outside his window for a few more minutes and enjoy that rather than methodically fold up his socks? Or why not write a letter to someone. Or even a poem? Or think about sketching that jug on the table. But how time seemed to twist away then hurtle past when he needed it to obey him. At least it was cold weather, for in the summer the heat made being late a sweaty and arduous experience. He finally made it to Liverpool Street Station, bought his ticket and rattled his way to Bishops Stortford. This was his second visit to the Tennants of Orford House, his first having been Margaret's invitation for her daughter Ariel's birthday party in

November. He was invited this time for the Puckeridge Hunt Ball. A chaotic, late arrival was Humphrey's perennial calling card and, as his hosts, Nancy's parents came to realise, "characteristic."

~

Orford House in Ugley wasn't an ugly place at all and neither were the family. Agnes ensured that all was comfortable, orderly and well-run, just as Humphrey was used to. Yet Orford House bustled with people and life so unlike the sedate melancholy at Menton. He was greeted warmly on the steps of the house, ushered into the hall and shown to his room. The moment Humphrey opened his suitcase he realised disaster loomed. He'd left part of his evening dress in London and only half his white tie waistcoat and a solitary evening shoe had made it in. He couldn't very well pad about the dance in his socks. His brown brogues would have to do.

Although the Tennants were enthusiastic hosts, elastic and unsnobbish in their opinions of who might or might not be worth entertaining, they had never come across anyone like Humphrey. At one end of their spectrum was Nancy's friend Vagn Riis-Hansen, Oliver Messel's long-term partner who had enlightened her on "certain aspects of life" to which she had been "hitherto oblivious" - despite Derek Hill's flamboyant company in Munich - and who delighted the Tennants by staging uproarious theatricals at weekends. At the other end was Joachim von Ribbentrop who would sit talking to Ernest late into the night on the serious issues of Bolsheviks, Germany, saving Europe and possibly the world.

Generationally Humphrey was out of step with Nancy and her siblings. He was far closer to Ariel in age, being 24 to her 19. His pacifism was something Margaret and Nancy could identify with, but his impulsive, devil may care exuberance less so. She described it as "hat over the windmill." He wasn't from the same mould as their cross-dressing cousin, Stephen Tennant, draping himself over chaise longues or posing with his lover, Siegfried Sassoon, for Cecil

Beaton photographs. Nor was he a man's man like Ernest. But Humphrey was warm and unselfconscious; perhaps it was these character traits that Nancy liked so much in the beginning. As the household and its guests recovered from the ball the morning after the night before, and plans were being laid for the day ahead, Nancy noticed him. He may have been scatty and chaotic but his enthusiasm, although "unusual" was gloriously life enhancing. A visit to nearby Saffron Walden was mooted: a favourite outing for Orford House visitors. It ordinarily involved a walk through the Cromwellian streets, admiring its place in history and the charm of its higgledy-piggledy architecture. Not so with Humphrey. Never had a guest insisted on manically climbing the Saffron Walden Church spire and forensically exploring every "nook and cranny" of the town. In a shop, he found a large blue and white tea and coffee set, which he couldn't afford but simply had to have. He persuaded Nancy to share the purchase with him.

~

Humphrey appeared in Nancy's life at the same age that Bunny had disappeared from it. Here was a young man, erudite, passionate about art, music, poetry and peace. He embodied what Nancy had missed for so many long, lonely years. The "flowery lot", seemingly wiped out after the 1914 Henley regatta, hadn't entirely vanished after all. Had Archie Middleton not died at Ypres, the man Nancy might have married would have been more than twenty years older than this vibrant, impulsive individual. But in 1933, Humphrey was alive, present and wanted to be her friend. He offered to paint her portrait. As well as exploring Saffron Walden that weekend, he had found an Edwardian velvet tea gown hanging in a wardrobe. It was a stately purple and had been given to Nancy by its previous owner, Mrs Dodd. Naturally Humphrey began referring to the garment by that name. Might Nancy wear 'Mrs Dodd' for a portrait and sit for him in London? Would she consider it?

Edwardian tea gowns had been, in their heyday, a sensual garment. Trussed up and corseted Victorian and Edwardian women could slip into this flowing unstructured robe to entertain guests, who were often male, in their boudoirs around four or five in the afternoon . . . hence a tea gown's illicit reputation; not quite a nightgown, a tea gown could, if desired, be removed easily for amorous assignations without the help of a maid ordinarily required to release her mistress from the strictures of a corset. So, the image of Nancy dressed in such an item with all the connotations that this implied was quite extraordinary. But Humphrey's imagination was filled with the nostalgia of Bloomsbury and here was his very own Vanessa Bell. It was imperative that Nancy come to Bloomsbury and sit for him in his studio. It would be easy. She was frequently in London, anyway, staying with her sister for part of the week. She could arrive at his "digs" in the morning, sit for a few hours, then take a break halfway through the day and go out to lunch. He knew a delightful little place round the corner where they could have a three course, "one and sixpenny" meal and then go back to the studio to sit again. Nancy began to spend "long delightful days" with her new friend. Not simply sitting for a portrait, but visiting friends, concerts and exhibitions with him. What a contrast with the rigours of the work she did for the NFWI. The wheels of her life were beginning to turn on a new axis.

In February, marital tragedy struck Margaret once again. Her second husband, Jim, died suddenly of a heart attack. The now middle-aged widow was left with Ariel in her late teens and three younger children. Humphrey offered to come to Orford to alleviate the intensity of their grief. He may not have felt close to his own mother, but he could certainly empathise and extend the tender hand of friendship. Unlike so many men at that time, Humphrey was unafraid to show his feelings. Nancy took note.

Nonetheless, the Bloomsbury sittings continued, and went on for months. Humphrey invited Nancy away to the Cotswolds, to stay in the primitive stone cottage he rented in Bisley close to Albert Rutherston, his old art tutor. It was enchanting. The tiny garden was "stuffed with lilies, snapdragons, bergamot and roses," recalled Nancy. The scent on a warm summer's day was heavenly. Evenings were spent "listening to Wolf Songs, and Mozart Quartets". Together they explored the misty, romantic landscapes of Ludlow, Chepstow and the Welsh border, where Humphrey's artist's eye and extensive knowledge of poetry amplified the experience into far more than just a country ramble. They immersed themselves in the beauty of the green and pleasant land that surrounded them. By the end of 1934, Nancy concluded that it had been the happiest year of her life. Humphrey wanted to share more. Could they consider a trip to Italy? He knew his way around Europe and, more importantly, realised by then that he had found the perfect travelling companion.

CHAPTER TWELVE

A Perfect Cicerone

1935

*"It was a new world to me and
new way of looking at the world."*

As a fair skinned Scot prone to sunburn, Nancy at first thought
Italy and the South of France might have been best avoided in
high summer. She then remembered it would be balmy and beautiful
at night, and the light, for Humphrey's painting, would be divine.
Together they began to plan a six-week trip for August and September,
catching a train from Victoria, a ferry to France, travelling down
through Italy and touring the art and architecture of Sienna, Assisi,
Urbino and Orvieto. They could visit Humphrey's parents too as Le
Clos du Peyronnet was so close to the Italian border. It was a standard
itinerary for two like-minded souls interested in art, music and beautiful architecture, but the fact that they decided to travel alone together
was an anarchic step. For the more Victorian members of the Gairdner
and Tennant families, it was at best, odd.

~

In May 1935, Nancy turned thirty-eight. She was a mature woman. Other women of her age and class, if they had married before twenty, as was the convention, might be launching their eldest debutante daughters into the London marriage market. Not only that, but Humphrey was a highly eligible contender in that market as a potential son-in-law. Handsome, well-educated with a private income and the heir to a grand villa in the South of France, in 1935, a fresh-faced, eighteen-year-old girl could do a lot worse. Here was Nancy, about to go on an extended holiday with a twenty-five-year-old, single man. There would be no female companion to keep the gossips at bay. Humphrey may have been sophisticated, fluent in French and Italian and a perfect tour guide, but the fact remained, they were an unmarried couple, travelling around Europe together and for six weeks.

It may have looked risky as far as convention went, but for Nancy, it was irresistible. And why shouldn't she go? She was grown up enough and was taken seriously in her own right. She had travelled independently in America, Canada and Europe. She had spoken at the League of Nations on peace and disarmament and was contributing to a seismic shift in the way women perceived themselves domestically and politically. Now she was simply choosing to visit Italy with someone who felt similarly about his surroundings. For Nancy knew there was much that Humphrey could teach her. She wasn't prepared to cast this opportunity aside just because of what society might think.

Nancy arrived well ahead of time at Victoria Station because she did not like being late, and found a couple of seats on the train. She settled down to wait, excited at the thought of the journey. But as time crept by there was no sign of her companion. She continued to wait. Perhaps he had been delayed, or maybe he had got the day wrong? She couldn't exactly set off without him. She ought to disembark. Standing up, she lifted her suitcase down, and stepped off the train back onto the platform, feeling decidedly deflated - this was not the seamless departure she had imagined. Suddenly there was Humphrey: striding down the station platform "in a rather lordly way" chatting happily with what appeared to be travel agent who was telling him "I've got your reserved carriage, sir." What a relief. They boarded the train, settled into a private carriage and began their journey in unexpected luxury.

Humphrey hadn't reserved the carriage, he had simply turned up in a rush, had been mistaken for someone else and happily played along. He hadn't forgotten the train time either, arriving on time, feeling pleased he wasn't late, then realising he hadn't got his passport. Back to the Bloomsbury flat he rushed, retrieved it and hurtled back to meet Nancy. He had packed hurriedly, cramming far too much into a suitcase that was far too small. As they disembarked at Newhaven, making their way to the ferry, Humphrey's hastily fastened suitcase exploded, scattering its contents. Hair brushes, sponges and sets of pyjamas were strewn across the platform. Fellow passengers picked their way through the jumble of possessions as the pair, scarlet with humiliation, gathered up the debris. Not much apology, but this was travelling the Humphrey Waterfield way: chaotic, slapdash yet all right in the end.

～

Even today, a train from Dieppe to Sienna takes nearly twenty-four hours; for Nancy and Humphrey it would have been far longer. The heat built up as they journeyed south, down through Paris and on to Italy, arriving in Sienna late at night. Nancy felt exhausted but she was going to need her stamina. They would be in town for a week, and it wasn't a languid week of strolling romantically through the fairy-tale streets. They had arrived for the crowded, noisy August

Palio. Waking early on her first Siennese morning, Nancy flung open her bedroom shutters. It was just before dawn and barely light, and as the sun began to rise, the cathedral materialized in front of her. "I was transfixed by seeing what appeared to be 'The Holy City, New Jerusalem coming out of Heaven.'" The dawn melted from "translucent green to rosy, pink."

~

Sienna's *Palio* hasn't changed in centuries. Each *contrade* or district, is represented by its own horse. Racing round a temporary track in the Piazza del Campo, the horses and jockeys look like a crazed bunch of bandits. No saddles or stirrups are used, it is man and beast doing the best they can together, using balance and horsemanship, flesh on bone. Their *contrade's* horse was an old mare, who wore a straw bonnet trimmed with pink ribbon and looked very demure as she was led up the aisle of Santa Catherina Church to be blessed before the race. Along with hundreds of Italians who piled into Sienna for the *Palio*, Humphrey and Nancy cheered and moved with the crowd. At the end of the race, sweaty and victorious, the winning jockey, stripped off his top and like a glorious flesh and blood Apollo, was raised on the shoulders of his comrades, cheering and drinking in the triumph of the moment.

~

Travelling with Humphrey was revelation. "It was a new world to me and a new way of looking at the world" said Nancy, and however chaotic Humphrey was with his personal organisation, he was present, loving, kind and above all sparkling with energy and life. In Humphrey, Nancy had found, "a perfect Cicerone". Chatting in French and Italian, imbued with art history and the imagination of a true romantic, Humphrey guided them both as they drifted from town to town, Duomo to gallery. The tour was not luxurious as aesthetics and the budget took precedence over comfort. Preferring authentic *pour tourists sans pretention* pensiones, Humphrey liked to get up at dawn when the traces of pink were still visible across the sky, and the cool of the morning allowed for greater ease of travel on an early bus. His ability to combine the academics of art history with pure visual enjoyment was a sensorial and aesthetic revelation. He and Nancy immersed themselves in the beauty of Tuscan architecture, walking the steep hills of San Gimignano, and staring out from the top of the hilltown across a golden landscape of olive groves and cypress trees. They whistled back through time to Byzantium and the sixth century, admiring the glittering mosaics of Ravenna and the monastery of Monte Oliveto Maggiore, clinging to its vertiginous cliff edged position. Together they admired the tender peace of Piero Della Francesca frescoes in Arezzo, with Humphrey describing the sight of La Mangia, the distinctive tower of Sienna, "as that marriage of pink brick and marble that sways as the clouds pass behind it, so like a water lily at the end of its pink stalk," said Nancy. They took in Gubbio, Urbino and Rimini. *'What stayed with me forever was the pottering about. There was nothing and nobody to come between us and our looking,'* she wrote. Humphrey was her guide, and they didn't need anyone or anything else.

~

After a month in Italy, they headed for the border with France and to Menton. It was time to meet Humphrey's parents. As they walked up the steep drive towards the villa, it felt like the perfect conclusion to their trip. The tumbling collection of the spice-coloured townhouses of Menton circled the bay, the sea looked still and serene, the steady bleat of cicadas filled the air and it felt as if they were arriving in a secluded paradise. Barbara and Derick were standing on the terrace to greet them, but before they were able to shake hands, let alone embrace, the visitors were asked to enter through a side door and gargle antiseptic. This was the rule for every single visitor to Le Clos before entering the house.

~

By 1935, Barbara and Derick were living in what felt like an Edwardian convalescent home. Betty Duff, the Scottish governess turned house-keeper, who had arrived at Le Clos when Humphrey and his brother were boys, was still employed and had become essential to Barbara's veneer of normality. Each morning, before Barbara and Derick rose for the day, the loyal, discreet housekeeper walked from room to room, on all floors of the villa, spraying the air and the surfaces with disinfectant. Humphrey's mother was now a *malade imaginaire*. Her fear of 'killer' germs had become an obsession and she believed she was protecting her husband's delicate chest from re-infection. But he was perfectly well. Barbara was really protecting herself from her own intrusive thoughts. Reality and the outside world were too forbidding. While Derick played tennis and croquet and even enjoyed a light flirtation with a younger woman in the town, except for her commit-ment to occasional good works and exclusive social gatherings at the Le Clos, Barbara spent hours lying in her ribbon festooned bed on the second floor gazing across the steady blue of the Mediterranean, longing for more affection than she received, drifting in and out of medicated sleep.

~

Nancy was introduced to Mario Lavagna, the gardener and groundsman. Born the same year as Nancy, he had worked for the Waterfields since his mid-twenties when the boys were young. His work of greatest splendour was the wisteria, a small creeping thing when he had first arrived but now a glorious leafy waterfall, cascading down the facade of the villa. The air was balmy, there were apricot trees and aromatic mimosa: the garden was a vision of a Mediterranean paradise. The scent of sun-warmed lavender, rosemary and cypress trees mingled with the smell of the sea. The villa's cloistered interiors were as elegant as the garden that surrounded them. Large floor to ceiling French windows, facing south, led onto balconies on three floors, a grand marble staircase at the back of the building provided staff with discreet entrance and exit from the main rooms.

~

Cool and elegant the interiors may have been, but Humphrey loathed the inert atmosphere. The fractured love his mother had shown him as a child had made him self-sufficient, and not in need of her attention. Nor was he able to pay Barbara the consideration she craved: he had little to share or exchange with her. In stark contrast with buoyant family life at Orford House, Humphrey's distant relationship with his parents was at painful odds with Nancy's adoration of hers, especially her closeness to her mother. The marriage blueprint for Agnes and William Tennant was nothing like the dutiful melancholy of the Waterfield's. "Scenically it was perfection but there were stresses and strains caused by Barbara's invalidism and it was not a happy home," said Nancy.

Having said that, Humphrey's parents welcomed Nancy warmly and did their best to behave as if their son's companion was entirely what they expected. But Nancy felt uneasy, almost apologetic. She was hardly the young debutante they might have expected him to find. Barbara could have even regarded her as a rival, a substitute motherly figure who had far more in common with her son than she had ever enjoyed. With the perfect manners typical of their generation, the Waterfields supressed any whiff of disapproval they might have felt, or even concern that their son was investing time in a relationship with a woman fourteen years older than him. *I shall always feel deeply indebted to Humphrey's parents. His mother cannot have liked the situation, but she accepted both it, and me with great kindness. His father realised I think that Humphrey was happy and conventions meant nothing to him. Had they made difficulties I should have felt I ought to fade away,'* wrote Nancy.

Barbara's emotional disconnection contrasted starkly with the warmth of her extremely demonstrative son. Humphrey railed against his parent's world, sometimes openly, blistering with anger at the torpidity of his family home. He loathed the formal, indolent pace of his mother's life, the painstaking planning of meals for her cook to produce and boring, genteel gatherings that constituted a Menton social life. He found his father easier company. They were, in some ways, cut from similar cloth, sharing a love of art and classical history and a determination to wrestle intellectually, whether lateral or based on rigorous scholastic precision. Yet his father could at times, exert control over his eldest son. One of Humphrey's teenage travel journals, in which he wrote his thoughts and pronouncements on civilization and literature, shows Derick's pencil annotations. While stopping short of grading the text, it demonstrated his need to oversee Humphrey's intellectual development. Unfortunately, the outcome was that, for Humphrey, 'family' meant a living claustrophobia trapped within his parents' stifling domestic arrangements.

~

Away from the villa, however, the Riviera days in 1935 were lovely, the nights heady and starlit. They went to the ballet in Monte Carlo, "with marble halls and exotic flowers", motoring back to Menton along the coast as darkness fell, "we drove home in the warm dark blue evening with twinkling lights looking like a fantastic necklace all along the coast."

Nothing had prepared Nancy for the bliss and joy she felt with Humphrey. Was he feeling the same, she wondered. Maybe, this unconventional "hat over the windmill" man would do things differently if it made him happy. Having been deprived of so much contemporary male company in her late teens and early twenties, and approaching middle age, she had finally found *joie de vivre*. Miraculously it was not with a grateful middle-aged man, possibly widowed with a clutch of children in tow, but with a vibrant, young intellectual who was in every way her soulmate. She had waited nearly two decades to find him. By the time they returned to England they felt like a couple in the first flush of romantic love.

1. Left: William and Agnes Tennant on their 50th wedding anniversary, 1936, in front of the commemorative gate that bore their initials.

2. Above: Orford House, the Tennant family home in Ugley, Essex.

3, 4, 5 and 6. The four Tennant children, clockwise from top left: Ernest, Charles Alan 'Bunny', Nancy and Margaret.

7. and 8. Above and right: the formidable Gairdner sisters, photographed in 1896, each holding the work that signified her particular accomplishment. The same group reassembled in 1936, Agnes is seated middle row, far left.

9. Left: Margaret with her first husband, Archie Mercer, the first of the family to enlist in the First World War, tragically killed in Iraq in 1914. Their child Ariel, was born posthumously.

10. Right: The Tennant family in front of a haystack at Orford Home Farm. William had originally proposed to Agnes 'on top of a haystack'. This typifies the informal warmth of the family. From left to right: Margaret, her second husband Jim Birley, William, Ariel, Agnes and Nancy, seated.

11. and 12. Left and Below: Hagley Hall, Rugeley, Staffordshire, where Barbara Waterfield was born and where Humphrey and his brother Anthony spent many of their school holidays, under the care of their Great Aunt Meta.

13. Above: Le Clos du Peyronnet, Menton, purchased in 1912 when Barbarba inherited a fortune from her father, having decided the English climate too cold and the Indian heat too dangerous for Derick's weak chest.

14. Right: Barbara, Anthony and Humphrey in the Long Pergola at Le Clos, 1913.

15. Far left: Barbara Waterfield in 1905, just before her marriage to Derick.

16. Left: Barbara and Derick at the bathing hut, Menton Lido, 1914.

17. Above left: Fun in the sun, Humphrey and Anthony were put to work in the garden early on.

18. Above right: Derick on the lawn at Le Clos with the boys.

Surrogate mothers.
19. Far left: Anthony and Humphrey with their adored governess, Betty Duff, 1915.

20. Left: Humphrey with Great Aunt Meta, who looked after him during the shorter school holidays, at Hagley 1920.

21. Far Left:
Humphrey's leaver's
photograph Eton, 1926.

22. Left: Humphrey at
Christ Church, Oxford,
where he achieved the
highest degree in
History for his year,
1930.

23. Left: Nancy in 1930, already beginning her 'ascent
through the Women's Institute heirarchy.'

24. Bottom Right: Nancy's first visit to Le Clos in 1935.
Both she and Humphrey look equally ill-at-ease.

25. Bottom Left: Albert Rutherston, Humphrey's art tutor
at the Ruskin, Oxford, with Humphrey at Le Clos in 1938.

The making of Hill Pasture 1936 - 39.

27. and 28. Left and Below: Humphrey surveying Erno Goldfinger's revolutionary design for the house at Hill Pasture which began to take shape in 1937.

29. Below Left: Mr Reynolds, the gardener who had offered his services after wandering up to inspect what all the commotion was about and enquiring as to 'what fool had bought that medder.'

30. Below Right: Nancy and Mr Reynolds, under the willow tree that grew beside the spring which was the only source of water in the early days.

31. Above: The Chase in 1937. Humphrey teasingly referred to it as Nancy's 'model piggery' and stayed there frequently. During the war Nancy returned to Orford House to stay with her parents.

32. Right: Humphrey outside the Chase in 1937 with one of his paintings which was included in the only exhibition he ever held, in 1962.

33. Above: Humphrey after being accepted for the Friends' Ambulance Unit following his tribunal in Bristol, 1939.

34. Above: Nancy and Humphrey at Orford House, 1939, with Humphrey in the FAU uniform, having completed training in Birmingham.

CHAPTER THIRTEEN

The Cougar

1936

"Reprehensible and immoral."

Nancy stretched out in the sun on the balcony of Le Clos feeling its heat flood through her body. She gazed out to sea. It was all perfection. 1935 she concluded, had been, quite simply, the happiest year of her life. So far, 1936 was measuring up nicely. The elevation of the villa and its proximity to the shoreline gave an impression of it hovering above the Mediterranean. Nancy recalled "I still remember the rapture of lying on the balcony watching the palm tree waving its pale green plumy leaves against the sea and the wisteria climbing along the balustrade." She and Humphrey had returned to Le Clos for Easter and for Nancy to recover from a bout of 'flu. Mario's wisteria was in full flower, its honeyed scent hanging in the air, the sky was the brightest blue, and she could smell sea salt. As she gazed at the beauty surrounding her, she knew she couldn't rush back to London. She was just so happy where she was. "Demoralised by pleasure, I rang the WI office and told them they must find a substitute for the work I was to do the following week."

Back at Orford House, Nancy's mother, Agnes, assembled for a family group photograph with her sisters. Brothers were not included in the portrait, for this was about the Gairdner daughters only. This later photograph was an exact replica of one taken at Broom House when Agnes and her sisters were in their teens and early twenties. The youngest, Lucy, still a child, wore a frilly pinafore dress and sat on the floor, her hand resting on a black and white terrier. The older sisters, including Nancy's mother, were dressed as grown-up women. They wore well fitted, high collared dresses, and further up the age range, corseted gowns. Looking confidently towards the camera, each one of them holds an object highlighting her respective capability. Jessie, the eldest, holds a violin, Agnes, embroidery, her sister, Anna, a book. Whether they are knitting, playing music or reading, they were shown as spending their time in a seemly, productive way. These were wholesome, virtuous young women, certainly not lounging about waiting to be seduced.

The sense of Scottish propriety and industry pervading Agnes's Gairdner photograph makes an interesting comparison to the way her contemporary Tennant cousin-in-law Pamela Wyndham appeared in one of the most lauded portraits of its time. John Singer Sargent's Edwardian fantasia, *The Wyndham Sisters: Lady Elcho, Mrs. Adeane, and Mrs. Tennant*, described as "The Three Graces" by the Prince of Wales, was not simply a triumph of artistic talent, it provides for us today, a window onto how privileged, desirable women were expected to look. Mrs Tennant, who had married Nancy's cousin, Edward, sits with her two sisters in a frothing sea of feminine sensuality. Swathed in silk and chiffon, with plenty of skin on show, there are no props to denote their individuality apart from their facial features. Nancy's branch of the Tennant family in future, would barely meet the en-nobled Glenconner side, now infused with the 'electric' Wyndham genes and swept into the most exclusive social circles in England.

Years later in 1935, while Nancy was touring Europe with Humphrey, the now middle-aged Gairdner sisters re-assembled, still holding the same props. Anna Gairdner, was now a double aunt to Nancy and her siblings, having married Nancy's uncle, John Tennant. Two of the corseted, sensible Gairdner sisters, Anna and Agnes, had married two Tennant brothers, John and William, and they had had eight children between them. Their sense of propriety had not changed. Although a hint of a smile danced across the faces of some in the group, they still appeared serious, with a prevailing air of bespectacled blue-stockinged worthiness.

In the summer of 1936, Nancy and Humphrey embarked on a far more ambitious trip: nearly two months touring Greece and Turkey. They would begin their journey at Le Clos. Just as the Italian tour had been joyful, their foray to Asia Minor would prove to be no less magical. It was, according to Nancy, '*another revelation of happiness and beauty: the Parthenon at sunset, scarlet anemones and Mozartian goat bells at Mycenae and Humphrey's extraordinary gift for enhancing every experience.*' Unfortunately, no-one at home truly rejoiced in her newfound happiness. Nancy returned to England to her scolding aunts, who viewed her gadding about with a young man as "reprehensible and immoral". It was not the behaviour of a Gairdner woman of the formidable photographs. She had brought shame on herself and her family. Although she was thirty-nine years old with national responsibilities requiring intelligence and thought, Nancy was informed, "for the first time, the family copybook had been blotted." She felt no judgement from her father and sister, they were unconcerned but her mother found her youngest daughter's behaviour distressing. She couldn't understand the relationship and she couldn't understand Humphrey. He was strange and different. He seemed extravagant in a way the Gairdners were not. Nancy may have protested it was platonic but her mother didn't believe her. It simply didn't wash, and Nancy had to concede that from the outside, it didn't look like that to her either.

A life without Humphrey would be diminished and joyless - she couldn't break it off and didn't even want to think about it. She described the conflict between family loyalty and love for her mother with her desire to stay with Humphrey as being "torn in two". Nancy was not the first or last woman to appear more invested in her romantic life than the man she had fallen in love with. The contrast of a young man in his mid-twenties at the start of his adult life embracing everything and everyone he is free to enjoy, with a woman staring middle age in the face, who has lived as a romantically disappointed adult for two decades could only conclude in one of two ways. Marriage or bust.

~

Like many relationships in the first obsessive flush, everything was easy, and no searching questions were asked. The energy of mutual delight and discovery propelled them deeper into their affections and shared interests. The idea of Nancy being a predatory seductress was ludicrous but it was the stereotype that fitted. Throughout history women like Mae West, Princess Margaret, Lady Randolph Churchill, even Shakespeare's wife Anne Hathaway who all took younger lovers or husbands, were branded as wild and 'other'. Today, mature women who partner with younger men provoke comment but nowhere near the controversy they used to. The stereotype of a wily woman of experience, longing to satisfy her desire with a younger man was, in 1935, prevalent. Was Nancy one of these women? Of course not. But that was the impression given to the starchier members of her Scottish Protestant family by her mother.

~

Homosexuality, although illegal until 1967, was quietly tolerated within the social circles where it was able to express itself. In pockets of society and certainly on the margins of Nancy's family, it was an open secret. The gay men that Nancy knew of were her cousin Stephen

Tennant, Pamela's son who lived his gender-fluid life openly and flamboyantly, Derek Hill the artist and the theatrical Vagn, the good-looking Dane and companion to Oliver Messel, who had already opened her eyes to the notion of love between men. So, she was not ignorant of what homosexuality was, but had not applied that label to Humphrey. Why would she? He was, by her own admission, affectionate and physically 'demonstrative.' In an era when, for a well brought up girl, a chaste kiss on the cheek was the physical limit prior to the wedding night, it was perfectly understandable to assume that marriage would be the endgame. *'We were constantly together, despite increasing opposition from some quarters, and I rocketed between bliss and disappointment certain only of one thing that this miraculous companionship was worth any price.'* She was certain that, after almost two years, it was time to tie their colours to the mast, however unusual – because of the age gap and not because of any physical preference - it might seem. Humphrey's mother was a little older than his father. Perhaps that was what the Waterfields preferred.

CHAPTER FOURTEEN

Love and Marriage

1936

'Miraculous friendship.'

The letter confirmed the bombshell. There would be no marriage, no conventional romantic conclusion. In all the time Nancy and Humphrey had spent together, it hadn't crossed his mind. *'My dear One, I hope you are better. I cannot bear to think of your beautiful white drawn face made miserable on account of me. I owe so much to your love & companionship, and I cannot overstate what they have meant to me during the last year. I wish it had not been such one-way traffic. Your admiration and interest in my work, your kindness, your devotion, I wish I had been more sensitive, more perceptive.'*

~

Nancy and Humphrey spent the evening in tears. He had been blind. Too young, too excitable and too selfish to see what he had done. When a friend pressed him on what the future held, it triggered romantic disaster. Of course, he couldn't marry her, she was far too

90

old. They were just very good friends who had a rejoiced in a "marriage of true minds". He had felt liberated by their friendship: they enjoyed the same things, they adored each other. But she was never going to be his wife. He would marry a young woman, one day. He hadn't met any he wanted to marry yet but that would be, naturally, the likely course of events. Wives were young and glamorous. A man got married when he felt ready to "settle down". Humphrey had no desire to settle down to anything in 1936. He wanted to paint, to travel and to create. He loved her deeply of course, but only as a friend. He didn't desire her. He had entirely misread the situation. It was a proper, heart-breaking mess.

~

The blissful weeks of European holidays, hot balmy nights, hand holding, walking arm in arm had been simply companionable affection regardless of how new and romantic the experience may have felt to her. No expectation should have been read into his demonstrative behaviour. He felt ashamed and appalled at his lack of awareness and he was devastated he had hurt her. Romantic disappointment had bruised Nancy in the past but this was different. Humphrey had transformed everything. He felt like her rightful companion, her best friend, her greatest love. This remarkable companionship couldn't simply be cast aside if he couldn't fulfil the conventional trajectory of romantic conclusion. There would be nothing that could possibly replace it. A split would leave her heart-broken and what would she gain? Yet existing in a twilight world of holidays and theatre trips felt like the territory of a mistress or an upbeat school chum. They meant more to each other than that.

Humphrey wasn't even sure if he believed in the concept of love and marriage. It was too constricting, too prone to failure and disappointment. He had not grown up with any archetype of expansive marital joy in his own family. Somehow Nancy's age had given him the freedom not to have to think about it and tying himself down to a predictable future. The agony was what to do with their intense feelings for each other. Neither of them wanted to walk away. Humphrey was happy to appear eccentric and unconventional, but Nancy just couldn't. She may have broken down barriers and expanded horizons for women, but that was within the acceptable frame of the Women's Institute. If she couldn't honestly expect to marry him, she determined at least to remain his friend, his very best friend. She couldn't give him up. Rather than making him feel guilty or somehow cruel, she would set him free. Free to be himself, unfettered by worldly cares and commitments. That could be her expression of her love for him. She took comfort and inspiration from the poet, Rilke, '*her gift of herself she wants to make immeasurable; that is her happiness. And the nameless suffering of her love has always been this: that she is asked to limit her giving.*'

Could that possibly work? Could he accept that? It was a profoundly generous position to arrive at on her part. Humphrey wasn't heartless, quite the opposite, he may have been lacking in his empathetic field of vision, but he did love her. '*But it is no use regretting anything. Remember my dear I am yours to command. I have got over the first sense of tragedy and can, I think, in the mood you so bravely adopted last night, only hope it was genuine, not a great effort. I only want to do what is best for you. But I daresay it would be well not to meet for a week. I shall miss you very much. Love H.*'

In the 1930's, close friendships between unmarried women and men were considered, without exception, suspect. Sex had to be going on. Why else would a man want to spend all his time with a woman unless he wanted to sleep with her? He could go to his club for companionship and conversation with members of the same sex. If he was much younger than the woman he was friends with, it was just plain odd. As much as Humphrey and Nancy admired the artistic talents of the Bloomsbury Group – Nancy enjoyed reading Virginia Woolf, she even said only Woolf could have adequately described the beauty and melancholy of Humphrey's parent's villa in France – they had scant knowledge of the sexual ambiguity of its members. Nancy was nothing like Virginia or her sister Vanessa Bell. Humphrey wanted to be an artist but would have recoiled at the thought of emulating the libidinous, bisexual Duncan Grant.

A week after Humphrey's letter arrived, they agreed they could try to set disappointment and misunderstanding aside and meet for a walk. For a recently fractured couple, they still walked hand in hand like a pair of innocent young lovers under leafless beech trees together. Their future had to hold something tangible if marriage couldn't be the answer. They needed an alternative plan. Within weeks of their romantic *denouement,* Humphrey made the decision that would affect the rest of their lives. He was going to leave London and move to Essex. He was going to buy a house or land or both and live near Nancy. For someone who didn't love a woman enough to marry her, Humphrey's behaviour defied logic. He could have stayed in London or bought a tract of land anywhere. He had no real connection with Essex except to Nancy. Explaining his decision to any prospective Mrs Waterfield that, putting down roots close to another woman who loved him deeply, was going to be impossible. How would Nancy be able or expected to bear it if he eventually did marry someone? The truth was that Humphrey knew it would never happen.

~

Ariel found the land at Broxted initially, which was a run-down field. Newly engaged, she and her fiancé, John Crittal, were looking for property too. It was no good for them because they needed a house, but perhaps Nancy and Humphrey should go and have a look at it?

The land for sale was a sloping paddock, off a small lane in a tiny village. The two friends arrived in Broxted one late summer's day, entered through a gate and stared at a funny looking meadow. In front of them was an unloved three-acre plot that had been used as the village rubbish dump. Coarse, unforgiving couch grass was the main feature and where it hadn't run rampant, there were great thickets of knee-high stinging nettles. However, the position was perfect. Looking west, the view from the lowest point of the field was truly lovely: a gently rolling English landscape of interlocking fields and hedges spread over the Pant valley; the sunsets would be spectacular. Turning east, a copse of ash and willow met their gaze. Shelter would be provided from the cold East Anglian wind and tender plants could flourish beneath them.

~

Humphrey liked it very much. For him, it was like looking at a blank canvas, waiting to be stretched over a wooden frame, placed on an easel and brought to life. This piece of England's green and pleasant land might be a forlorn field today, but tomorrow it could transform into his dream garden. When Humphrey lost his childhood paradise at Hagley Hall, his heart had been broken for the first time. Now these acres offered consolation. No longer need he fear the transient scent of summer honeysuckle or freshly turned hay smelling truly sweet for a few moments in the summer sun. He could grow his own plants, plant his own trees and savour the beauty of nature in his own permanent space and in perpetuity. As the seasons changed, he could look forward to the plants he had grown reappearing again, having enjoyed the season just gone. He could travel backwards in time, retracing the painful steps that had taken him away from his childhood Eden in Staffordshire, arriving at an English paradise of his own. But unlike the solitary little boy who had played in the gardens of Hagley and suffered their loss, he was no longer alone. He had Nancy to hold his hand.

~

The village of Broxted hadn't changed much through the centuries. Set in what appeared to be a rural backwater, the winding lanes and cottages of the original hamlet centred on the pretty thirteenth century flint and brick St Mary's Church. Ancient hedgerows lined the roads.

So unspoilt was it, that Humphrey made up his mind to buy the Broxted meadow almost immediately. In September, he obtained permission to dig from the local council, and as the sun was still casting its golden rays, throwing long shadows as it sank below the expanse of peaceful green, the field that had been the village dump began to transform.

CHAPTER FIFTEEN

Paradise Found

1936

'A heavenly bit of our life.'

Cherry trees, roses, lilacs, poplars, ilex, catoniastas: Humphrey and Nancy chose plants as the images of what the garden might become streamed through his mind. While the diminutive whips and saplings they chose looked small and unappealing in their fledgling state, Humphrey knew how they would evolve aesthetically and the practical, physical benefits they would provide. His creative imagination began to reassemble the landscape he had lost. Hagley may have been demolished and the garden expunged, but he was now free to create his own 'paradise' with the woman he loved. It was the same for Nancy. There was now a justified reason to be with him, as often as possible. What could be more straightforward and morally sound than creating a garden with a friend? *'It is difficult to describe the excitement and joy of those October days when we first started the garden. We had no water except for the spring under the big willow and no shelter except for a hay stack. It was a heavenly bit of our life,'* wrote Nancy.

96

Nancy and Humphrey planned and planted through the autumn of 1936. Living the Ruskin dream that the principal role of the artist is truth to nature, their hands, heads and hearts worked in unison. Breaking for a picnic lunch, they would lean against the haystack surveying their new world. This earthly paradise would be called Hill Pasture. The name evoked a painterly beauty and played on the pastoral ideal; a Romantic Imagination fused with the permanence of earth and simplicity. There would be a house too, as Humphrey felt he couldn't carry on staying with Nancy at Orford indefinitely. He wanted something simple and modern. He had met a young architect, Gerald Flower, an assistant to Momo architectural legend, the volatile and difficult Erno Goldfinger. Flower drew up some plans - the house would be a small bungalow: modern and brutally plain. With nature's beauty surrounding it, the building would be a window onto the world and not distract. It wasn't long before Erno Goldfinger himself seized the project and took over; the temptation to make a complete break with the past was too great. For this house would never be Hagley or Le Clos, it was going to be simplicity itself. It was an invitation to look beyond architecture, without the trappings of Edwardian splendour, offering an entirely new way of thinking about living space.

Erno Goldfinger was certainly an acquired taste in character and architectural style. Born in Hungary, he studied and worked in Paris for a decade before moving to London in the early 1930's. Having initially trained in architecture and furniture design, in London he turned his whole attention to modernist architecture. His sensibilities were entirely Europolitical, and even today his work is divisive. Some are evangelical about the bold simplicity and honesty of his creations, delighting in the recent Listed Building badge of honour being applied to some of his work. Others find his Momo style a miserable representation of Brutalist, Communist inhumanity. Ian Fleming loathed his architecture so much that he named a Bond villain after him, ensuring Goldfinger's posterity but possibly not in the way the architect would have wished. Notting Hill's Trellick Tower and the penguin pool at Regent's Park zoo are two extant examples. The house at Hill Pasture was his first domestic building project and was an unashamedly modern creation. The house was based on squares and *'derivatives of squares'* wrote the architect James Dunnett, in a letter regarding Hill Pasture. *'As a courtyard house, it is perhaps unique in British architecture projects . . . Goldfinger told me that the spatial effects on entering through the door in the brick wall were his most direct architectural expression of Surrealism.'*

"The house was a statement. It was a conscious experience. It was a 'perfect villa,'" says Lynne Isham current Hill Pasture owner and architect, "It was not designed to be a place of traditional domesticity. It was a house for one person, maybe two, certainly not a family." For a one bedroomed block of a house that had a modest footprint, it wasn't cheap. It cost Humphrey £750 to build, at a time when the average salary was £153 per annum. The position of doorways, passages and windows were planned to direct the visitor to vistas beyond, where the views from the house presented like a gallery of three-dimensional landscape paintings, ever changing with the seasons. The house offered glimpses of tradition and familiarity but then subverted them. In spite of the simplicity of stark plain walls and architrave free window frames, there was to be an inglenook fireplace containing a small window which looked onto the garden. There would be no holing up in a fireplace avoiding the world. However bright or bleak the landscape, however leafy or leafless the trees, nature would find you. This was to be a place that let the landscape in, rather than battening down the hatches against it.

Like a Picasso collage, expectations and associations would be both fulfilled and denied. It was not a place of scale and dominance, rejecting as it did the Palladian or Georgian hauteur of a traditional English country house. Nor was it anything like the ornate, marbled exteriors of Le Clos, towering majestically above Menton. Hill Pasture felt like open house: a democratic invitation to engage and participate.

The views would also go on to inspire Humphrey's painting style, his compositions of the natural world would alter and evolve in colour and form as he watched the seasons sweep past the huge, frameless windows.

Entrance to the house was through a simple colonnade of steel and timber, covered by a corrugated roof. The airy sitting-room-cum studio, filled with light all day, could be divided into sections with a curtain. The terraces and courtyard would offer up views; enclosed courtyard walls were constructed to arouse curiosity, manipulating the visitor to wonder what might be round the corner. Clever, avant-garde and contemporary as the architectural design of Hill Pasture was, for an Essex countryside planning committee it was utterly incomprehensible. They thought it so ugly and strange that permission was only granted on the condition it would be invisible from the road. Which meant more landscaping was required: more plants, more ideas, more creative opportunity and much more fun.

Humphrey's vision for the garden design was influenced by Lawrence Johnstone's mix of formal and naturalistic planting at Hidcote. Gertrude Jekyll, who in turn had been influenced by Turner and Impressionist artists was another inspiration. The composition had to be as compelling as engaging with a painting. The visitor's eye would be drawn from the lower part, where the house would sit, up past the soon-to-be-planted cherry trees and magnolias. Up and away across the space, the eye would travel, guided by a 'ride' or 'walk', which would be an avenue of thuya hedging. He and Nancy named it Chatsworth. Chatsworth was to grow to wide enough to feel like a generous walk, and also form points of interest or secret gardens along the way, concealing then revealing small formally planted areas and mini gardens. That autumn Nancy and Humphrey dug in fifty squat little whips of the fast-growing evergreens. Nancy bought quantities of a single variety of the palest cream rose, the sweetly scented Moonlight Hybrid Musk. They were her first 'present' to the garden. They were to line the Chatsworth walk on the right-hand side, creating a simple palette of whites, creams and green.

The autumn of 1936 merged into winter. One evening, as Humphrey was attempting to put up a fence, an old man ambled up to see "what fool had bought that medder," introducing himself as "Mr Reynolds." A local man, he was illiterate and disapproving of twentieth century's new-fangled ways. Then surprisingly, he offered to help. He had in his possession a prized "bagging hook"- perhaps his skilled use of it would be useful to the "young master?" Soon, Mr Reynolds became indispensable; he may not have been able to read or write, but his countryman's knowledge of flora and fauna proved invaluable as the garden took shape. A true disciple of the old school, he refused to move his clocks to summertime hours, declaring "God's time was good enough", rising when it was light and going to bed at dusk. Under his expert management, the field began to concede to whips and lawn. Little by little, the couch grass retreated, the stinging nettles were expunged and the structure of the garden began to emerge.

~

In spite of the size of the field, Humphrey's initial vision for Hill Pasture was on a much more modest scale. He imagined a small formal area of cultivated garden running between the two thuya hedges. But the more they cleared, planted and surveyed again, the more his imagination began to soar. It was as if he was taking a step back from his canvas, scrutinising the composition and then going in again with more colour, shape and direction. Cherry trees suddenly seemed right, so they were added. Another evergreen hedge went in, this time yew, it would give a line of deeper shadow. Shrubs planted against the yew would provide further texture. Six screening poplars were dug in to line the small drive area, with cotoneasters beneath, offering the interest of delicate bunches of tiny white blossom in spring and bright red berries in autumn. An orchard was planned for the front of the house, with lilac trees at the back. Humphrey found it easy to draw on his vivid, visual imagination but when he tried to communicate his ideas, it was often to a baffled audience. Even Nancy struggled to see "what he was getting at" at times. The field was now a depressing mess of mud, grass, sticks and whips and looked worse than it had ever done as the village rubbish dump. Humphrey rushed about when explaining his plans to bemused visitors, dashing from spot to spot, enthusing madly about the splendours of the future. "Photographs of this period show how bleak it all seemed at first. Humphrey with the beauties to come in his minds' eye would, waving his arms, ask puzzled guests to admire the rows of labels poking through the grass." explained Nancy.

~

Rather than drawing plans, he and Nancy placed six-foot canes at intervals across the property. She stood with a feather duster strapped to a broom, patiently standing in for a tree, a shrub or any other composition in Humphrey's mind's eye, as he adjusted exactly the right place for the next sapling using the landscape beyond as his guideline. "He seemed to know by instinct how to mould his design into the lie of the land," said Nancy, "and would stride about, sticking canes in here, pulling them out there . . ." For wholly practical reasons, Humphrey favoured soft muted colours and low maintenance shrubs and trees rather than the back-breaking work required by the lavish herbaceous borders of the Victorian gardens he had grown up with. Hill Pasture's maintenance would be as modern and straightforward as the lines of the Goldfinger house.

~

In the grey depths of winter, when the trees were finally bare, Humphrey stood in the field surveying the scene. With his hands thrust into the pockets of his Oxford bags, his crumpled tweed jacket worn and shapeless with use, Hill Pasture felt recklessly extravagant for a young man still in his twenties. Perhaps it was. But he couldn't allow the joys of childhood and Hagley to evaporate into the past. Owning the nearest thing to a living canvas which could revive the past had to be worth it.

~

The promise of better things to come encapsulated in a slab of land in Essex was in stark contrast to the world beyond, where cracks were beginning to show through the solid ice of the status quo. There was still honey for tea, and a patrician prime minister, Baldwin, who gave as much priority to fly fishing as to the contents of his red box. But as 1936 drew to a close, belief that the 'war to end all wars' was beginning to feel foolishly optimistic. Europe was restless. As Nancy and Humphrey battled with twitch and nettles in the autumn sunshine, the Nazi Party banned the Hebrew and the alien word "*Halleluljah*" from prayers in all German churches. By November 1936, Benito Mussolini had referred to an "German-Italian axis" in a speech. And just after lunch, on the 11th December, after a few tense and disorientating weeks, King Edward VIII abdicated and left his country forever to marry Wallis Simpson. In deepest Essex, however, Christmas was still lovely and after attending Midnight Mass, two figures could be seen wandering by moonlight in a muddy, sloping field on the edge of Broxted. For Nancy and Humphrey at least, paradise endured.

CHAPTER SIXTEEN

In Arcadia Ego

1937

As the New Year dawned, so did the desire for another blissful trip to Europe. With Goldfinger's work on the house at Hill Pasture progressing well, Nancy and Humphrey planned another, more ambitious adventure. It would be the longest yet, two months starting in France, travelling on to Italy, Greece and Turkey, and this time in spring – to avoid the heat of their first voyage. Nancy certainly needed the respite. She was now being paid for her full-time commitment to the NFWI in her role as Music Organiser. She had accelerated her activity with the Associated Countrywomen of the World (ACWW), by spending the last few months travelling up and down the country. In spite of the heartbreaking discovery that Humphrey had no intention of marrying her, the prospect of spending weeks alone with him was impossible to resist. Why would she give up time spent with someone who brought so much fun and friendship into her life?

∼

The trip began at Le Clos where Easter was spent once more in the soporific elegance of the Waterfield villa. They left for Italy by boat from Marseille and sailed south to Naples. First stop was at Caserta, the colossal Baroque palace built as a seat for Italian kings. The scale and pomp of Versailles was its inspiration, and outside, described at the first 'landscape garden' in Europe, were endless walks, lakes and temples. Miles of cascades descended to a series of pools and fountains and an 'English garden' covered twenty-four hectares alone. The scale was overwhelming and all Humphrey's garden fantasies were played out on an unimaginably grand scale. Together he and Nancy looked and absorbed. The principles and beauty of the place, its perspectives and how the light played on the water lodged in Humphrey's mind to apply to something of his own. Spending far too long admiring the wonders at Caserta made them late. Screeching back to Naples, racing through the battered streets with their distinctive smells of drains, sea and food they almost missed the boat. Nancy was getting used to these last-minute panics, caused by Humphrey's desire to squeeze every last moment to the limit. The next stop was Athens.

~

Humphrey insisted on waiting until sunset before visiting the Acropolis when it was far more beautiful and atmospheric. He knew the sky would imbue the marble of the Parthenon with its luminous scarlet and orange colours. Afterwards, the couple sat together on their hotel balcony, enjoying the view and discussing the news from home. Good progress was being made; the whips, saplings and shrubs at Hill Pasture were growing steadily, plans for the house had been finalised, and builders booked. In the meantime, there they were, sharing another fabulous adventure. Their intertwined life felt blessed. After a few days in Athens, they travelled to the Peloponnese, arriving in Olympia in the early evening, *'dusk was falling as we wandered among the ruins where the fritillary was flowering all about . . . a huge white owl flew from behind a pillar almost brushing our faces. We felt we had had an encounter with Athene,'* wrote Nancy.

~

They spent ten 'halcyon' days in Mycene in a tiny hotel, built by the German archaeologist who had excavated the ancient site. How could life have transformed so completely in such a short space of time? Nancy's work in England was fulfilling and at times demanding but this friendship satisfied her emotionally. Their days followed a happy pattern, sight-seeing, painting, wandering. In another life she might have been a mother of several children, in the thick of domestic responsibility. Yet here she was, almost forty years old, staring across an ancient Hellenic landscape with a friend, her very best friend, close by. Of course, she knew, the relationship wasn't perfect. Sometimes, if she had been feeling braver, or less conventional, she might have wanted to abandon herself to it, but she knew she couldn't. He had made it plain that she was never going to be his wife. So, she consoled herself with the knowledge that for now, even if it could not be forever, their friendship could be savoured and treasured. One day he would marry someone younger, probably glamorous and beautiful. Why wouldn't he? He was a dream partner. Maybe the glamorous future wife might be as talented and unique as him. Perhaps Nancy would be godmother to their children. But for now, on this sunny Greek day, there was no sign of that at all.

~

'I loved wandering about on my own while Humphrey was painting. One day I was sitting on a hillside which was carpeted with scarlet anemone fulgen when a shepherd and his goats came tinkling by. Each bell had a different tinkle and it sounded like a Mozart sonata on the move,' she wrote. The pair moved on to Byzantium, to old Constantinople, recently renamed Istanbul, and Humphrey was enchanted by it. The minute he saw the skyline of mosques and

minarets he refused to stay in Pera, or Beyoglu, the 'European' side of Istanbul, the conventional choice for tourists. He wanted to be in the thick of the Ottoman quarter. Far more interesting to be close to the bustle of the Grand Bazaar, in the shadow of the Hagia Sofia, The Blue Mosque, The Sultan's Palace: in the beating heart of Ataturk's new Turkey.

~

Nancy didn't like it. Bug bitten and tired she couldn't agree. "I feel an absolute pall of cruelty hanging about the streets and the Sultan's palace," she declared. But Humphrey didn't think so, not at all. He liked the exotic beauty of the place, the warmth of the Turkish men, their open affection for each other as they walked hand in hand, arms tangled around each other in the streets. He liked the way they sat in their cafes playing backgammon, smoking and drinking apple tea - letting the day drift by. He was happy to wander the streets, stopping in the bazaars for tea and conversation. "Don't you realise you can actually see Santa Sophia from your pillow?" he pleaded with Nancy, to justify staying in their shabby hotel location as they walked mile after mile through the streets. A boat trip down the Bosphorus felt calmer. For Nancy, the return leg of the journey, back through Greece was a relief, as it "seemed more beautiful than ever."

~

By the autumn of 1937, the foundations of Humphrey's house at Hill Pasture had been laid and building had begun. The site was no longer a field with a messy line of twigs in a muddy bog, it had become a discernable layout. Next on the list was a peony garden to be positioned near the drive. Then sweet, citrusy *philadephus* would be dug in beyond Chatsworth and the emerging courtyard area was to be lined along a wall with *magnolias* and *stewartias*, white and cream, and white again, with punctuations of yellow to their floral centres; then even more white with *spiraras*. More cherry trees and then irises to line the path to the front door, with climbing roses added ready to sprawl over the walls. At the back of the house, Humphrey decided to plant a 'camellia court'.

~

In the same way that Humphrey's friendships could only be enjoyed in, as he put it, "single file" his planting was similar. He focussed intensely on individual plants, forensically studying them, until he understood everything about them Although he planted groups of one plant, he chose a variety of species within that group. Each one had reason to be there, so that information as well as aesthetic pleasure could be derived from admiring them. Why have one variety of magnolia in the magnolia garden if you could have five? He could enjoy them all "one at a time, in an orderly queue of individuality." On the 1st April, 1938, the house was finished, and Humphrey moved in. Barbara and Derick came to stay to admire their eccentric son's project. He rushed about the site, waving his arms vigorously, explaining the design, "seeing sheltering hedges, exotic plants and dramatic vistas, while they, shivering in the cold, only saw sticks and labels in areas of twitch." But it was already even better than expected and Hill Pasture was already a dream garden in his mind.

~

The summer saw another visit to Le Clos but the political climate in France had changed. A previously straightforward local Menton walk, crossing the border from France to Italy and back again into France was suddenly impossible. Nancy and Humphrey were surrounded by shouting Italian carabinieri in an olive grove, interrogated and escorted to the border. Barbara and Derick began to wonder whether remaining in Menton was a good idea. Life in Ugley was similarly uncertain. William, Nancy's father, was not well; cancer had been diagnosed which Agnes decided not tell him. The Liberal Tennant patriarch, the loving father and grandfather who believed in female education and independence was beginning to fade away. Soon there would be a new head of the family.

～

Yet Ernest was also suffering the effects of diminution, in this case to his reputation. His conviction that brokering a deal for the British Government with Nazi Germany to avoid war was being overturned. In early 1938, Ribbentrop had given up on Hitler's mission to befriend and mollify the British ruling class and had returned to Germany to become its Foreign Minister. Edward VIII's abdication had dashed any Third Reich hopes for an amenable pro-German king, and the Berlin Olympics in 1936, which were meant to showcase a brave new world of Teutonic athletics, had descended into a horror show of murder and anti-Semitic cruelty which had been denounced around the world. Ernest could no longer pretend, or even hope that he was able to influence anything at all. In September 1938, in his last attempt to be able to offer any insights in his capacity as Hon. Secretary of the Anglo-German Fellowship, he accepted an invitation to attend the Nazi Party Rally at Nuremberg. He was not the only Briton there. *'The large British contingent of visitors included several Peers, Members of Parliament and businessmen. The visit proved an alarming and depressing experience with Hitler and Goering screaming threats at the Czechs and defiance at the rest of the world . . .'* he wrote in his book *True Account*. For someone who considered himself as part of the Establishment, Ernest was now tainted by his association and friendship with Ribbentrop.

～

Meanwhile in that same month, Great Britain began to batten down the hatches. Although Chamberlain began his diplomatic peace missions to Germany, nonetheless London began to evacuate. In Essex, the local Saffron Walden mayor was told to expect three thousand East End children. Gas masks were assembled. Ernest's teenaged son, Julian, was sent home from school while his wife Noni created an 'anti-gas room' in their drawing room by plastering up all the windows, blocking the fireplace and piling the outside of the windows with sandbags. Margaret Tennant decided to leave England for Ireland, taking her children with her. On the 15th September she stood on the platform at Paddington station with Nancy and their father to see off the 'sad little party'. Just as their train was about to pull in, there was an announcement. Chamberlain had secured an agreement with Germany after the first of his peace talks. War appeared to be averted. Relieved, Margaret and her children returned to Ugley.

~

For those that overlooked the obvious ruthlessness of the National Socialist German Workers' Party in the early 1930's in the hope that appeasement between Britain and Germany would prevent war is even now, regarded as misguided. Yet with Chamberlain's arrival at Heston aerodrome announcing the Munich agreement, it seemed, for a short moment at the end of September 1938, that the dreams of Ernest Tennant's Anglo-German Fellowship had been realised. November brought different news. When the horrors of *Kristallnacht* were not only reported but photographed, and when German concentration camps expanded to imprison not simply political enemies of the Nazi party but its religious and ethnic 'enemies' too, Ernest's hopes and dreams came crashing down forever. The Edwardian summer of Henley 1914 and the world it represented, would never return. All that remained to him were the London offices of the C Tennant & Co, hunting and butterfly collecting.

~

In France by the end of the year, another way of life was becoming increasingly destabilized. The Waterfield's secure and charmed Menton existence was under threat, because even before the official start of the war, tensions on the Italian French border had begun to scare them. Nancy and Humphrey's unpleasant encounter with the Italian carabinieri in 1938 had been a warning sign. Barbara and Derick could hardly bear to believe it, but it was increasingly risky to live so close to Mussolini's Italy. The world had changed around them. Living in the place that had once been a retreat, the warm, exotic micro-climate where their sons had grown up and regarded as an intrinsic part of their identity, was not sensible or safe. Le Clos remained a large, beautiful villa, but it was no longer a sanctuary. When Germany invaded Czechoslovakia in March 1939, Barbara and Derick left.

~

Like many of their English neighbours, at first they had wondered to where to go. A winter in England with Derick's weak chest, as far as Barbara was concerned, was out of the question. They required somewhere warm. Pau was an obvious choice. It was grander than Menton, and was filled with rich, European aristocrats who had established the English Club of Pau at La Place Royale. Subsidiaries of the club were the reassuringly exclusive polo, golf and hunt societies, open only to Anglo-Saxon families of pedigree. Inland from the Atlantic, near the Spanish border and the Pyrenees Mountains, the climate was not as humid as the Mediterranean but was warm enough. The Waterfields moved into a smart townhouse, La Jouvence. For Barbara it felt like the choice between the devil and the deep blue sea. The last thing she had wanted was to leave Le Clos. She didn't like travelling anywhere very much and to abandon her familiar, elegant surroundings for the unknown, however beautiful and stately, felt like another loss.

CHAPTER SEVENTEEN

Broxted Loam

1939

"We seemed to have buried our heads for too long
not in sand but in Broxted loam."

A grim new reality was beginning to bite. War was coming and for any young man physically able to fight, it meant conscription. Humphrey would have to either enlist or think of an alternative. In just under three years, Hill Pasture was already evolving into the little Eden he had imagined for so long. Lying stretched out on the summer lawn of what had been a scrubby field, gazing out west across the valley with the scent of philadelphus and tree peony in the air, military mobilisation seemed impossible to contemplate. Instead, he and Nancy decided on a summer jaunt to Italy and France with a visit to a Spanish painting exhibition in Geneva where they would soak up Goya, Velasquez, El Greco and Murillo.

~

As the summer progressed, the stifling weather in England seemed to match the oppressive political mood in Europe. In early August, a heatwave sweltered over London. Joyce Tennant, married to Nancy's cousin Bill, moved from room to room in her house in Camden Hill Road trying to find a cool spot, thankful to know she was going to the west coast of Scotland for the rest of the month. Her son John was playing in Kensington Gardens with his nanny, her eight-month-old baby, Malcolm, was sleeping. It was a moment of quiet. She lit a cigarette. But peace was not coming to her home or anyone else's. The previous December, the first of 10,000 *Kindertransport* children had arrived in Britain, signalling the beginning of a mass exodus from Germany. Within two years, her home would be abandoned. Bomb damaged and unstable, the only relic of her family's pre-war existence were the salvaged oak panels that had lined their dining-room walls, stacked up in the back of an old shed, riddled with woodworm.

∼

Such gloomy thoughts, thus far, hadn't intruded on Nancy and Humphrey's holiday. The exhibition in Geneva had been lovely they agreed, as they sipped champagne on a hot summer's night in Nancy. They were leaving the following day, heading west to Barbara and Derick in Pau. But the next morning they got up to find their hotel abandoned. The manager and all the young men in the village had left overnight. Shocked, the pair realised this was not going to be the carefree tour they had enjoyed in previous years. They progressed through France, staying first in Le Puy and then on to Rodez feeling increasingly uneasy. Europe was disintegrating. It would be safer, Nancy decided, for her to return to England by train while the railways still appeared to be running normally. Humphrey would see if he could reach his parents by car. If war was declared, he wouldn't be seeing them for months and if they couldn't get to England, maybe years.

∼

As he drove through France, Humphrey reviewed his options. War felt inevitable. But should he really fight? He would be terrible at it. He couldn't even catch a train on time. He had been a committed pacifist since his days in Oxford and hadn't changed his views. When he reflected on the impact that the First World War had had, he knew that he and his contemporaries had lost the patriotic fervour of the young men who fought it, the 'flowery lot' of Nancy's youth and indeed her own brother Bunny. Disillusionment was the driving force of appeasement and pacifism. When he and his generation thought about the war, up came images of generals flushed with port, moving diminutive flags around a map on a billiard table in a country house drawing-room, plotting the decimation of thousands.

~

On the flip side of the coin, Pacifist men polarised opinion, particularly generationally. Somehow it was more acceptable for women to be peacekeepers, being naturally nurturing and mutually co-operative. Nancy's peace mission on behalf of the NFWI to Geneva was a case in point. Men, on the other hand, even if they weren't bristling, muscle bound warriors, should at least be prepared to defend their women and children from a marauding enemy. A true pacifist would not fight. What sort of man was that? A few years earlier, on 9th February 1933, The King and Country Debate at the Oxford Union had rocked the nation. Students at the Union debated the motion, 'This House will under no circumstances fight for its King and country'. The motion had passed with a resounding victory. It was a far louder echo of the similar debate at the Cambridge Union in 1927. As news of the Oxford students' vote filtered out, it was viewed as both a national triumph and outrage. *The Daily Telegraph* ran the headline: "Disloyalty at Oxford: gesture towards the Reds." *The Daily Express* didn't simply suggest it was Communist to vote for the motion, it declared pacifism appealed to a transsexual, weak and idiotic sort of human being, '*There is no question but that the woozy-minded*

Communists, the practical jokers, and the sexual indeterminates of Oxford have scored a great success in the publicity that has followed this victory.'

∼

From a young age, Humphrey had been steeped in the War Poets' polemic. The poetry of Siegfried Sassoon, Wilfred Owen, Rupert Brooke and Osbert Sitwell sympathised with and helped form his perspective. At least a decade or even generation younger than those of who had fought and lost their lives in the trenches, he nevertheless felt drawn to their politics and sensibilities. They were men like him, and Humphrey had written, in 1928, his own eulogy to their bravery:

'You were the first of all our band
To tread the dark uncertain way
Alas, that ours should be the land of light
And yours the house of clay!'

∼

There was nothing particularly unusual about his desire for peace. The Tennant family in their different ways, represented much of the national mood: Ernest's revulsion and fear of a bloody history repeating itself in a Bolshevik takeover; his sister Margaret campaigning for the Peace Ballot. The British people, to a greater or lesser extent shared these sentiments. In May 1935, Neville Chamberlain declared in the House of Commons, "we know that in war there are no winners. There is nothing but suffering and ruin for those who are involved." Plays like *Journey's End* made no bones about the futility and heartbreak of war loss. There were numerous pacifist organisations spanning all sections of society and parts of the country, but registering as Conscientious Objector catapulted a man into very different territory. Many people disapproved. It was perceived as subversive, self-indulgent and feeble. Public opinion perceived pacifism as not supporting the status quo, potentially allowing collusion with the enemy. Against such prejudice, for pacifists to take a public stand required real bravery. Humphrey would need to draw deeply on his convictions and accept the disapproval of contemporaries, family members and worst of all, veteran soldiers. But he had the confidence of the outsider in knowing there were alternative ways to be and live.

～

Humphrey was a fast driver, so much so that Nancy found his speed and ebullient style of motoring nerve-wracking at the best of times. Now he needed to travel at warp speed. He had managed to see his parents, they seemed to be well enough even if more downbeat than usual owing to the political climate. Back on the road north to Dieppe, there would be no slacking to gaze on a sunset or drawing a curve of a river while admiring the trees and flowers - freedom to travel where and when he wanted now felt strangely fanciful. There was a nervousness in the air. As he approached the port he realised he was not the only one trying to leave in a hurry. Luckily for him his little Morris was small enough to get on the boat and was last over the drawbridge. The travel gods had saved him once again. On 3rd September 1939, Britain declared war on Germany.

～

Once back in England, Humphrey and Nancy stepped up their planting. Three years exactly after the conception and creation of Hill Pasture, time was now of the essence. Humphrey needed to plot the co-ordinates and then Nancy could fill in the spaces. They planted more and more. Chatsworth was extended so that six holly hedges would go in to continue the wall of the courtyard to the magnolias. There had to be more roses, 'old fashioned' roses in the garden proper, with a yew box planted at the back. They added more cypress, more philadelphus, more magnolia and more orchard.

～

Before the summer, Humphrey had met and become friendly with two young Quaker pacifists, Nik Alderson and Sandy Parnis. They were living in Thorley, a village near to Hill Pasture. Humphrey had no intention of becoming a Quaker on religious grounds, he was agnostic, but he could see a way to contribute to the war without fighting. He particularly liked Nik. Charismatic and good looking, he seemed a contradictory mix of authoritative masculinity and pacifist conviction. In early October 1939, Humphrey registered as Conscientious Objector, and attended an Exemption Tribunal in Bristol. He could still contribute to the war effort by caring for the wounded. The appointed judge at the Bristol Tribunal, Judge Wethered, was particularly impressed by the Quaker equivalent of the Red Cross, The Friends Ambulance Unit. At least they were offering a practical, humane alternative war effort. Humphrey's application was accepted and his fate sealed. In November, he received a letter from the FAU, requesting he report to the Quaker philanthropic HQ and training ground at the house of Dame Elizabeth Cadbury near Birmingham.

～

Nancy and Humphrey had one week left together before he had to leave. Forlornly she watched over him as he packed up their "happy little life". His paints, brushes, canvases and easel would have to lie dormant until who knew when. But the garden would carry on. Nancy would make sure of that.

Although it was a wrench to leave Nancy and Hill Pasture, Humphrey delighted in his newfound male companions most of whom were intellectual, musical and bookish. In a group photograph of the Birmingham training group, Humphrey beamed into the camera, his thick mop of longish hair betraying his lack of interest in the traditional short back and sides. He exuded the same joyful ebullience as the sailor-suit clad boy in the garden at Le Clos with his father and brother years earlier. Now he was flanked by two beautiful young men of which there were several in the group. Nik Alderson was one of them and a new acquaintance, Peter Townsend, was another. Tall, athletic with thick dark hair and piercing blue eyes, Peter's good looks were matched by a fierce intelligence and intellectual curiosity. Like Humphrey, he had studied history at Oxford and his brother was the talented painter William Townsend, the future Slade Professor of Art. An intense friendship was struck, to the extent that Nancy would later refer to him as 'your beloved Peter.'

CHAPTER EIGHTEEN

Scandinavian War

Spring 1940

'I desire to live to go on painting, to watch the trees at
Broxted grow to something like maturity, to see the cherries
and magnolias bloom, to see my friends again and England.'

The Norwegian soldier glanced inside the abandoned ambulance
but there was no-one in it and nothing to see. Then something
caught his eye. Picking it up and turning it over in his hand it
appeared to be a simple school exercise book, surprisingly heavy, with
a flexible black canvas cover. He opened it. There was something
written on the top right corner: *'D H Waterfield Finland April 12th'*.
Page after page was filled with stylised handwriting in black fountain
pen. Greek sigmas and extravagant flourishes curved up and down
the feint-ruled paper making the writing extremely difficult to read.
It seemed to be English, but of an archaic nature. The pages looked
like a gothic manuscript, an ancient fairy story peppered with a few
dates. It seemed too precious to throw away or leave behind. It might
mean something to someone, its owner, if he was still alive, or his

family, if it was an account of his final weeks. It wasn't until 5th of May 1940 that the Norwegian soldier handed the black, canvas journal he had found in the empty ambulance to a Swede called Erik Wiklund. Erik had a friend, Stig, who had an English wife. Perhaps she could do something with it, or at least be able to decipher its flamboyant scrawl.

⁓

Ordinarily, early May in Norway was cause for celebration. The snow, even in this northerly part of the country, had melted, swelling the rivers and waterfalls, flowing down to the fjords and out to sea. Apple blossom was out and migratory birds, flying back for the Scandinavian summer, chattered in the trees. But the scene at Namsos was one of bleak destruction. The once thriving market town situated on a peaceful bay, was strewn with metal and broken vehicles. Wooden houses had been bombed and burnt to oblivion. Humphrey's ambulance containing his lost journal wasn't the only abandoned vehicle on what remained of the quay. As German artillery fired from the land and sky, the Allied troops had retreated. Some of The Friends Ambulance Unit (FAU) had managed to leave with them. It had been a tense decision. Either the FAU unit retreat from Norway, back through Sweden, possibly to remain stuck in Scandinavia for the rest of the war as POWs: or rush to the Allied evacuation and flee across the North Sea under cover of darkness. The FAU chose to depart from the Norwegian coast. It was a frightening and unceremonious way to leave a place that had provided such a warm welcome only a short time before.

⁓

Three months earlier, Humphrey and twenty-year-old Stephen Verney had been selected to form part of the FAU Scandinavia mission. Aristocratic and erudite, Verney was the perfect driving companion for Humphrey, as each ambulance required a two-man team. An

Oxford Classics student and musician, their delight in each other's company was mutual.

"I drove an ambulance with a lovely man called Humphrey Waterfield, an artist, a cultured man. We were quite a fragile lot of people in our inner personalities and all going rather against the grain of the world for that time . . ." said Stephen Verney in later years. Verney had not been born into a Quaker family but, like Humphrey, had attended a tribunal and on the basis of his convictions, was accepted. As secure in his beliefs as Humphrey was, Verney didn't care for following the herd either. Training at Dame Elizabeth Cadbury's house was a real endurance test. This group of pacifists may have passed their tribunals on the basis of their objections to war, but they also had to be as fit as their fellow soldiers.

The Unit completed its training in just over two months, rising in the dark for uphill runs as the dawn broke, and practising driving the heavy lorries and ambulances and support field hospitals with Red Cross medical training. Musical scholars rubbed along with naïve public school boys who in turn rubbed along with working class men. It was convivial, broke down class barriers, and demonstrated how manual skills were as valuable as the academic ability to strategize: *"We were an extraordinary mixture of academics and practical people, this was very good for us academics, [as we came to learn] it was much more important to be good with your hands rather than ancient Greek history . . ."* Freddy Temple.

~

The FAU's role in Scandinavia was to support Finland in the 'Winter War', also known as the 'Russian Finnish War' when on 30th November 1939, Russia arbitrarily invaded eastern Finland, citing historical ownership of the land and the need to defend Leningrad only 30km from the border. The FAU's services were accepted to help move the wounded and homeless civilian population, who had fiercely resisted the Russian invasion, to safety. They were to work alongside the Red Cross, wear Red Cross uniforms and drive their lorries and ambulances. Theoretically at least, thanks to its internationally recognised emblem of neutrality, the Red Cross could keep out of harm's way. But the physical challenges were harsh. The men were to endure long dark days and the continuous, bone numbing cold of a Scandinavian winter with little or no sunlight, sometimes sleeping like the Swedish army on branches of pine to prevent hypothermia, with a small wood burning stove in the centre of a tent. If they were lucky, from time to time, they might find themselves sleeping in a bed kindly offered by local Finns.

～

In early March 1940, Humphrey's FAU convoy departed from nearby Loughton, where the Unit had been put to work in the hospital, and by happy coincidence, drove through Ugley on its way to Newcastle. Nancy couldn't resist one last romantic gesture. She wrote out the words to Mozart's *Magic Flute* farewell chorus, and threw it into his ambulance as he drove past. Now Humphrey could hum something lovely even if he couldn't see his garden. But perhaps writing them in German might have been overdoing it . . . Prior to his embarkation to Norway, Humphrey would have to explain these hand-written opera lines to a suspicious customs officer.

～

At first the expedition seemed so comfortable it was almost comical. They spent the night before sailing to Norway in a perfectly acceptable "second rate hotel" in Newcastle. Food was plentiful and there were even generous helpings of rationed treats like chocolate to enjoy on their voyage. They arrived in Oslo to find a warm welcome, comfort and more good food. It felt like a peace-time holiday. *'Chiefly for its own sake we enjoyed so much of our stay in Oslo with its friendly people and happy lit up streets after English black-out'* wrote Humphrey. Not for long did the FAU bask in the warmth of such a welcome.

On 13th March 1940, the Winter War came to an abrupt end, with the signing of the Moscow Peace Treaty. For the next month, the Unit travelled across Sweden on to Finland: their mission was to drive back and forth across the frozen Finnish landscape, returning convalescent and refugee Finns to their homes.

~

Spring may have been raising its pretty head in the gardens of Essex, but in Scandinavia it was still very much winter, where March was the bitterest of months. After weeks of darkness preventing any sunlight warming the ground, the ice remained thick and the snow was at its deepest. Temperatures were as low as minus 40 degrees centigrade. As two hundred days of winter turned to spring, the thaw began; an event which made conditions even worse for the convoy drivers. Routes over frozen lakes disappeared and to remain on solid ice, the convoys had to detour further north, via the Arctic Circle. *'Gradually we lost our fear of the ice,'* wrote Humphrey, *'snow and skids seemed to obey a law of nature which would eventually be related to a determinist principle. Still, in the early days, 20mph was a good average.'*

~

Driving on narrow ice roads of the Finnish winter, with vertiginous banks of snow piled high on either side, required nerves of steel and the physical strength for which Humphrey and the Unit realised they had been trained. If a driver skidded, and his vehicle spun, he ran the risk of facing in the wrong direction. There was no opportunity to do a three-point turn, the roads were far too narrow, the hapless driver would have to retrace his journey, back along the road "to the jeers and amusement of the others" recalled Freddy Temple, sometimes for miles. Temple described the contrast between the bodily thermostats of driver and co-driver. 'It was hard for both the driver and co-driver. The driver would be in a muck sweat, terrified, with his heart pumping, insisting on the window being open, the co-driver freezing cold."

No one made the mistake of touching the sub-zero vehicles with gloveless hands twice. Human skin froze instantly to metal. After a while, they learnt to use skids to travel round corners and make use of the ice.

~

In the midst of it all, the beauty of the Scandinavian landscape was not lost on Humphrey. The difference in the night skies and colours of the Nordic world moved him. When he had moments to wander off, he was enchanted. *'The lakes stretched down long perspectives of low pine covered shores with small islands attractively disposed . . . a wonderful peace descended and consciousness returned . . . the first was the more beautiful, the black curve of water, the little boat drawn up among the snows, the dark shapes of wooden shacks on the foreshore. And at night, the peace of the engine silenced and the ferry moving through the water, the stars bright and it seemed to me, unknown beyond the Pole. Orion staggering home to bed behind the pine trees. It seemed the setting for the conversation on Immortality in War & Peace.'* Resentful of man's resolute march towards industralization, he railed against the sound of engines disturbing the peace of the landscape, *'The internal combustion engine, repulsive at best, is particularly unpleasant to be sentenced to in this country whose great quality it violates. If you leave the camp in the evening, beyond our clearing is a little farm where the sunset paints the most wonderful colours in the eastern skies, strange, exquisite skies.'*

~

On the 9th April, the political landscape changed again. German forces invaded neutral Denmark and Norway. News of the attack reached the unit. Suddenly it wasn't simply a question of operating what Humphrey regarded as an albeit worthwhile but hypnotically mind-numbing "bus service" and Stephen Verney called an "ambulance ferry service." The next phase of the mission would test their mettle. '*It is horrible to think of invasion & war having descended on that oasis and civilisation* [Oslo]. *Also, we were disturbed at the thought that we are quite marooned. We cannot hope for letters to and from home, we may be isolated here for the duration of the war, without power to do anything to alleviate the suffering....at the officers meeting tonight, April 12th, it was agreed that we stay. Meanwhile we carry on with the tedious, useful work of carrying out more or less bona-fide convalescent patients along the Finnish roads.*'

~

He felt slightly ashamed of his desire for real action over the monotony of the winter transportation service they had provided, but at least it would be something worth sacrificing his art and life at Hill Pasture for. '*I find myself excited at the prospect of war in Norway, unreasonably and wickedly, I know too it won't last. To risk death in a Norwegian spring seems less than the certainty I felt of death in a Finnish winter. The chances seem so much greater in our favour. It is not I think that I am afraid to die . . . and I have been a favoured one of our ghastly civilisation and hung like a ripening peach on a sunny wall storing up sweetness against the winter – it is merely that I desire to live to go on painting, to watch the trees at Broxted grow to something like maturity, to see the cherries and magnolias bloom, to see my friends again and England. But if war must be I want to see it, to have abandoned painting in order to drive a bus service is to be defrauded.*'

~

Initially, the unit continued trundling through the slowly thawing landscape of Finland and Sweden, in relative safety, occasionally having days off to relax and admire the "girls worth looking at." The eastern Swedish town of Lulea caught his eye. '*The landscape on either side of Lulea was the most paintable I saw in Sweden. Rows of pale red hurdles against this sky and lakes whose middle had dissolved to liquid turquoise . . .'.* But as spring progressed, German aggression increased: *'April 20th All day dismal accounts of what lay before us kept coming in. The Germans have control of the air. Not a house in Namsos stood, the French have lost all their food and there was little to hope for in that direction . . . a Swedish ambulance has been bombed. We spent the day on tedious little jobs about the cars, though I did find time to read Twelfth Night in the snow. The sun was delicious and as I woke up in the morning, I had a vision of Menton and imagined myself among white iris with the olive filtered sunlight falling on them. In this wonderful weather war seems ridiculous and not to worry about as if nothing could permanently scar the silence of the mountains.'*

~

News filtered out that a mass evacuation of Allied troops was planned from Namsos. The FAU split up. Some would progress to Namsos and try their luck at leaving with the rest of the troops, others would turn back to Sweden. Humphrey's unit made for Namsos, if they were lucky, they would make the planned evacuation on naval vessels bound for Scotland before the Germans army prevented it. *'At 11 pm our orders having come through to divide into 3 parties . . . between 1 and 2 we crossed the Norwegian border . . . we are sorry to leave Finland. We hoped to see spring and the summer lights, visit these northern forests to see what grows and what reflections live upon the waters. We hope the English ambulances will be long remembered. Three thousand people travelled by them, and, we hope through us, remember England with affection.'*

~

In the last days of April, Humphrey's Unit made its way into Norway. It was best to travel at night, when the temperatures dropped and the snow was sufficiently frozen to drive over. *'Stops were endless, I was always jumping in and out, blowing whistles and passing down messages which meant sometimes quite a considerable walk. To add to the excitement, we had to be on the lookout for machine guns or bombs from aeroplanes one had to decide whether a particular noise was a lorry or ambulance behind or in front – we went in two parties, five minutes apart – or an enemy machine, the danger was greatest at the top of the pass where the walls would have been difficult to scale and there was no cover from trees. We had martin hats ready and wore our white camouflage coats over our great coats. It was a hot, still night warm even at the top of the pass. The sky was a pale luminous blue and Venus looked over the low ridges of snow-covered mountain and the waste of snow in the foreground.'*

~

Inching their way over lumpy, frozen ground, narrow passes and vertiginous drops, they were peppered with machine gun fire. Wanting to believe it was a mistake, perhaps the Germans hadn't seen the Red Cross emblem from their planes, the Unit halted and scattered into the forest, waiting for the planes to fly away. They did. Humphrey was struck by the co-operation of the men. *'April 30th – May 1st. The last few miles were the worst. Just when we were at last arriving, we had to take to the woods for an aeroplane alarm. Aeroplanes have been busy all day . . . they spattered a village with machine gun bullets yesterday but they did not seem to make any effort to destroy it. The hills are wonderful camouflage: you can see no-one though you know there are at least ten men lying sleeping in the woods. I washed in the river in the morning and lay in the sun on the mountain all afternoon fast asleep half aware my face was burning but unable to summon the energy to move to shade. After our second night we were all pretty well tired out, pushing cars is heavy work on top of the driving and food rations were short. But I enjoyed it all. The patience of everyone was truly admirable and no lost tempers though people were in some cases too tired to react to the instructions they were given. I cannot help thinking that to get the whole convoy over the pass, without fuss and without accident or as far as one knows, material damage, was a very creditable achieve-ment.'* But there was no time for complacency. As the Unit descended to Namsos, it faced scenes of chaos. Crowds of British and French troops were massing, ready for withdrawal with whom the Unit were meant to be boarding, but there were no naval vessels in sight. The Norwegian coast was shrouded in heavy fog, and the British Navy was nowhere to be seen.

CHAPTER NINETEEN

Back from the Brink

May 1940

'We had a blissful week, even the nightingales
came to welcome him.'

O n 29th April 1940, Lord Louis Mountbatten left Scapa Flow
in command of four destroyers bound for Norway. The North
Sea was shrouded in thick fog. So often a deadly, disorientating
hindrance, on that particular cold spring day and on such a dangerous
mission, the obscuration was a blessing. The order to evacuate over
five thousand Allied troops had been given, and in Namsos the
formidable one-eyed, Major General Carton De Wiart was waiting
for Mountbatten's naval convoy to arrive. As it turned out, the heavy
fog was useful, but not useful enough. Mountbatten's ships hid in
the treacherous rocky shoreline shrouded in fog banks but their masts
betrayed their position: they could be seen from above. German
bombers descended. Mountbatten's flotilla pulled back further out
to sea, and then tried again.

Humphrey, Stephen and the rest of the Unit having arrived at

Namsos on the 1st May, were instructed to dismantle their ambulance engines. Humphrey refused. It seemed a waste of a good vehicle - it wasn't exactly a tank, but it could save human life, whichever side you were on, but the army insisted - they were doing the same themselves. Reluctantly the members of the FAU began to strip the machinery down. On the 3rd May, Mountbatten's destroyers docked and evacuation began at 10.30pm. At 2.30 am on the 4th May, they left the rocky Norwegian coast bound for Scotland. It couldn't have been more different to the convivial arrival in Oslo earlier that year, with the lights of the Norwegian capital twinkling across the water through the winter night. The May retreat from Namsos was dark, cold and frightening. Two hours after the final ship sailed away there was enough dawn light for German aircraft to begin an attack. A French destroyer, *Bison* exploded, killing one hundred and thirty-six men on board. Another ship, *Alfridi* picked up the survivors in the water who were being peppered with machine gun fire, but was then was hit by a heavy bomb and capsized leaving one hundred men dead. Stephen and Humphrey lay in the hold, packed in with other members of the Unit, troops and ammunition. There were no smoking signs everywhere but as soon as the first deep blast of a shell thudding into the North Sea was audible, the troops lit up. At least they would go down smoking a last cigarette. Luckily their ship didn't sink and they arrived to the "amazing sight of the green fields in Scapa Flow after a world of snow" remembered Stephen Verney. They were taken ashore and given large mugs of sweet tea, reboarded and finally disembarked in Glasgow.

~

Meanwhile Nancy had been busy in Wales with NFWI work. She had been travelling from house to house, accepting hospitality from other members in her capacity as Vice Chairman. One night she might find herself staying in a stately house, and on another in the terraced home of a mining family. Arriving at the door of yet another NFWI hostess, she was presented with a telegram. ARRIVED SCOTLAND

HUMPHREY. He had made it back in one piece, and so she hurried home. After so many weeks of no communication, they would be together again, reunited in the garden in beautiful, blossom-filled May. Humphrey arrived at Hill Pasture before she did. He had finally experienced the action that made war seem meaningful to him, and worth giving up this pastoral idyll. Now he was back, and in the place that made sense of everything. Even better, he had returned at one of the most beautiful times of the year. The countryside in front of him was in refreshing contrast to the frozen silence of an ice-bound Scandinavia; it was the peaceful, reassuring green of an English garden as it tipped from spring into summer. His Japanese cherry trees, *prunus amanogawa,* two tall columns of palest pink, prima ballerina *frou frou* perfection stood proudly against the sky. The box hedging he had lined the entrance of the drive with the year before, looked happily established. He was pleased he had decided to extend the *philadelphus* bed; it felt properly generous now. The pear blossom was mainly over, but the simple beauty of the apple blossom in all its variety of white, cream and sugar pink greeted him like old friends. The *magnolia grandiflora,* improbably exotic, dark leaved and glossy was doing well too, the strangely stippled buds still tightly closed, concealing a feast of lemony freshness for later in the year. In what felt like four short years the young man presiding over what once appeared to be a quagmire of unruly grass, whips and sticks had returned to Eden. Amongst the sweet scent of spring flowers, blossom and the sound of boisterous spring birdsong, Nancy arrived back.

∼

They knew they wouldn't have long together, most likely a week, before he would have to leave again and return to the Unit. But for a moment at least, they had each other, Hill Pasture and the seasonal beauty that surrounded them. Ordinarily they would have been content listening to Mozart or Beethoven on a gramophone in the evenings, but when darkness fell that week, they heard another sound and listened in wonder. Nightingales were singing from the nearby wood. It felt as if the most magical of British songbirds were rejoicing too, welcoming Humphrey home. Like a baby growing into a precocious toddler, the garden was developing its own character. Chatsworth was now a proper walk, with a mown lawn inviting a stroll. Because there was more structure, somehow the wilder areas suggested more inspiration. Perhaps the gullies could be used for creating something else, maybe a pond, or a sunken shrub walk? Nancy and Humphrey for that week, could talk face to face and plan. Of course, the views that surrounded Hill Pasture had the same steady loveliness they possessed when Nancy and Humphrey first walked into the field in 1936. The garden's beauty was safe in the embrace of the English landscape. But the sense of permanence was, of course, an illusion. Nothing was safe or certain anymore. For all the sweet nightingale song and apple blossom that greeted Humphrey and Nancy at Hill Pasture in early May, there was no escaping the realities of Hitler's ambition and the danger of the war becoming far worse.

～

On the 10th May 1940, the German army invaded Belgium, Luxembourg and The Netherlands. By mid-May it had advanced through the Ardennes region of France, cutting off French and British troops, forcing them back to the coast. By the time the Dunkirk evacuation took place between 26th May and the 4th June, the occupation of France seemed a certainty. German troops entered Paris without resistance on 14th June, and by the end of the month, France was under German occupation and the Armistice had been signed. After his May week in Essex with Nancy, Humphrey was off again, summoned to Gloucester, to work as a member of a team of hospital support staff. Leaving Nancy and the beauty of Hill Pasture was another wrench, but this time at least, he would be stationed in England.

～

He arrived at 100 Sherborne Road, Gloucester – a spartan house in a dismal street - and installed himself with other members of the Unit. He was put to work alongside Stephen Verney and other fellow 'conshees'. It was proper toil. Hours were "incredibly long" as Stephen Verney was later to comment. Night and day, Humphrey would stoke the boilers that powered Gloucester Hospital, while Stephen worked as a corpse porter. Other jobs included shaving the pubic hair of men who required surgery and working on the geriatric wards. The Pacifists were regarded with suspicion by some and downright aggression by others. It was particularly difficult when faced with injured soldiers who were beginning to appear in increasing number. Churchill may have made his stirring speech of fighting on the beaches, but the reality in a Gloucester hospital ward were rows of wounded servicemen, bitter and disillusioned. Looking a young maimed soldier in the eye as he lay in his bed, hoping to connect his disillusionment with the immorality of war was paradoxically difficult. The disgust shown for a pacifist's rejection of fighting was greater than the dreadful suffering experienced on the battlefield, and Humphrey's gradual realisation of this required empathy, humility and compassion. How distant now were the aesthetes who wandered among Oxford's dreaming spires.

～

As the threat of invasion increased, towns and villages in England began to prepare for war. Although Hill Pasture's garden remained under Humphrey and Nancy's care, the house itself was requisitioned by the British Army. Hardly a traditional stately home of vast proportions, offering gracious rooms for relocated boarding schools as many large country houses were, Humphrey's house was nevertheless a useful base for British Army troops, preparing for a possible invasion of the Essex countryside. By the summer of 1940 a German invasion wasn't just feared, it was fully expected. Nancy described how "farm carts were to be pulled across main roads, ditches were dug in the

35. Above: La Jouvence, the villa in Pau to which Derick and Barbara Waterfield fled in March 1939.

36. Right: In the garden at La Jouvence, May 1939. The following year Derick and Barbara were to take their own lives, fearing Nazi rule throughout Europe.

37. Above: The Friends Ambulance Unit (FAU) Second Company, November 1939, outside the 'Cadbury Barn' in the grounds of Brookside, the Quaker training camp set up at Dame Elizabeth Cadbury's house near Birmingham. Humphrey is seated front row, second from right in a cricket jumper. Stephen Verney blows the trumpet, and a skull and crossbones makes an unexpected appearance.

38. Above: The Winter War, or Russo-Finnish war began when the Russians arbitrarily crossed the Karelian Isthmus, claiming the need to protect Leningrad, 30km distant. On the Finnish northern front, active Finnish ski patrols operated throughout the bitterly cold conditions, December 1939.

39. Above: Humphrey's FAU was sent in after the Moscow Peace Treaty was signed in March 1940, to return refugee Finnish civilians to their homes. The ambulances leave Namsos for the Finnish border, March 1940.

40. Above: Conditions were treacherous, and driving the ambulances on the narrow ice roads of the Arctic Circle required nerves of steel and physical endurance.

41. Left: Namsos, Norway in April 1940, bombed by the Luftwaffe to smithereens. This was the sight that greeted Humphrey on his return as the troops waited for Mountbatten's fleet to arrive.

Graham Hughes. Peggy Hughes. Jay Birley. Linnet Birley.
1941

Mr Reynolds whose bagging
hook saved the garden during
the war. 1939 - 45. Mr Reynolds.

Nancy.

42. Above: While Humphrey was absent, Nancy made sure that work at Hill Pasture continued, roping in her nephews and nieces. Knowing that his creative vision was being realised, amid the destruction of war, kept Humphrey's mental health stable.

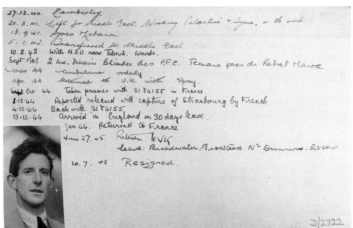

27.12.40. Camberley
20.3.41. Left for Middle East. Working Palestine + Syria, on the road.
13.9.41. Syria Lebanon
5.1.42. Transferred to Middle East.
10.2.43 With H.S.U. near Tobruk. Wards.
Sept 1943 2 hrs. Division Blindée des F.F.C. Temara près de Rabat Maroc
Mar 44 Ambulance orderly
Apr. 44 Returned to U.K. with Spray.
Sept Oct. 44. Taken prisoner with SI 84155 in France
1.12.44 Reported released with capture of Strasbourg by French
4.12.44 Back with SI 84155
13.12.44 Arrived in England on 30 days leave.
Jan 44. Returned to France
June 27. 45. Return to UK
Leave: Broadwater, Broxted. Nr Dunmow. Essex
30.7.45 Resigned

D/2722

43. Left: Humphrey's service record, detailing his subsequent movements with the Hadfield Spears in the Middle East, followed by France, capture and imprisonment in Strasbourg.

44. Above: the Hadfield Spears arrived in Suez to support the Free French army, May 1941. Humphrey is second from right.

45. Above left to right: Humphrey, Hamilton 'Hammy' Mills and Freddy Temple, Syria 1942.

46. Far Left: A significantly reduced Humphrey setting up the Spears' medical camp, Western Desert 1942.

47. Left: the Spears' mess tent, Humphrey bottom right.

48. Above: Le Clos du Peyronnet from above. After the war Humphrey and Nancy returned to begin the colossal task of restoration.

49. Above: The wisteria continued to grow for decades, lovingly tended by Mario Lavagna, the gardener.

50. Above: View uphill of the 'scala nobile' or central water feature designed by Humphrey, comprising of five descending pools running from the top of the garden down to a view of the sea.

51. Above: Humphrey connected the Mediterranean part of the garden with the Mexican part by planting arches of Italian Pencil Cypress.

52. Left: On the curved balcony at Le Clos, restored to paradise, 1956. From left Nancy's sister Margaret, then Humphrey and Nancy, gazing adoringly at each other.

53. Above: During and after the war Nancy continued with her work for the National Federation of Women's Institutes (NFWI), seen left attending a Singing Festival Ad-Hoc Sub-Comittee meeting in 1949.

54. Above: The culmination of two years of planning came in June 1950 at the Royal Albert Hall, with WI choirs from all over the country singing their hearts out, to Ralph Vaughn-Williams's Songs for All Seasons.

55. and 56. Above and Above Right: Work continued at Hill Pasture. In 1956 Nancy bought Ashgrove cottage and gave its land, which bordered Hill Pasture's, to Humphrey. He immediately set about planning the garden extension.

57. Right: 'Blissful' holidays were resumed, here Humphrey and Nancy are in Greece, 1959.

58. Left: In 1960 an additional storey was added to Hill Pasture, thanks to a neighbour's advice that Humphrey invest in television shares.

59. Above: The house terrace, abundantly planted so that flowers bloomed throughout the summer with perennial interest in winter as well.

60. Above: The covered walk, with iris borders and luxuriant plantings of roses, clematis and honeysuckle.

61. Above Left: The Long Walk, also known as 'Chatsworth' leading the eye to the vista beyond, punctuated by a series of small intimate gardens.

62. Above Right: The Moongate, created by Humphrey at the border of Ashgrove cottage and Hill Pasture. He manoeuvred Nancy around with a cardboard cutout, to ensure that the view from both sides was perfectly framed.

63. Left: Water, water, everywhere; the long pool in the iris garden.

64. Left: The legendary swimming pool, with its tumbling pergola of roses, scene of much joy for all the nephews and nieces.

65. Above: The Temple of Love, overlooking a small pond. Seated within, the contrast between the contrived order of the garden and the natural beauty of the valley below was a masterstroke of design.

66. Far left: Humphrey added an ornate, octagonal, lead tank with a fountain beneath a weeping willow. The grey of the lead combined wonderfully with the silvery green of the willow.

67. Left: 'The Last Painting, Thistles, Aug 1971' written poignantly by Nancy in her album. It was indeed Humphrey's last painting.

fields, while able bodied civilians were given instructions to walk westwards" in the event of an invasion. The defence plan was for Humphrey's studio window at Hill Pasture to be used for firing at the enemy on the road beyond the garden.

~

Germany now seemed unstoppable. Hitler's sights were set firmly on the British Isles but before that, on the 22nd June 1940, the Armistice between The Third French Republic and Nazi Germany was signed. From midnight on the 25th June, France was under Nazi occupation. On the 17th June 1940, Derick Waterfield typed a bleak but matter-of-fact letter to his sons. It wouldn't arrive until August.

La Jouvenance
17 June

'My dear Children
News of Petain's offer to surrender has come through, so that my defaitist (sic) letter of two days ago was justified in tone, although I did not think France would surrender so quickly, and probably so completely because Hitler will probably make the terms uncon-ditional. Then he will use the richness of France, its petrol and coal against England, which will be bombarded by a circle, and although I believe a quarter of the German aviators are dead, and a larger proportion of the best ones, it will be tactically very difficult to reply by bombardment of many hundred aerodromes any of which may be in use, at any time, while all the English aerodromes may be full and making targets. It could be done, England against the Continent as in Napoleon's time, but it will be bloody, and I am not sure whether England has the guts. If we could only get command of the air now instead of in 1941 or 1942.

If England goes on struggling, as it probably will for some months, we shall be more cut off from you than we are now. For a week we have had no English letters, no newspapers for weeks. I doubt whether the Germans would bother to insist on the French interning English subjects other than males of military age. We expect to get almost no coal or gas, the Germans will take it, but not at once. Whether they will apply Polish methods to France remains to be seen, they will certainly make it impossible, indeed they have already for France to fight them again, in fifty years. If you don't hear from us, it may be we are living quietly here, in some discomfort, or that we are caught and interned by the Gestapo, or that we have killed ourselves to prevent such a fate. But I don't think that will happen for some weeks.'

Within days they were dead. In a terrible repetition of the news of the deaths of her Tennant cousins and her brother Bunny in the First World War, word of the Waterfield double suicide reached Nancy first in a letter from the housekeeper at Le Clos, Betty Duff, addressed to Orford House. Yet again, Nancy would be the one to absorb and pass on tragic facts. She left for Gloucester with Betty's letter and told Humphrey herself.

CHAPTER TWENTY

The Last Resort

1940

'He often said the world would not be fit to live in.'
Betty Duff

It had been comforting for Barbara and Derick to see Humphrey briefly at the end of his last trip in the summer of 1939. A shame perhaps that Nancy had returned to England earlier: she and Derick were fond of her now; they could see that she was good for Humphrey, who seemed happier and more settled. Barbara smiled at the thought of their strange, clever, complicated son, chattering away about the exhibition in Geneva and how beautiful Hill Pasture was becoming; that had been nearly a year ago. Humphrey was now working in the Gloucester hospital and their younger son Tony, newly married, was training with the RAF. She had no idea when the family might ever be reunited. Barbara missed her sons and she missed Menton. She remembered that in June, the humidity of the town would be high. She longed for the strong steady blue of the Mediterranean with the view of the warm, spice-coloured buildings of the Old Town circling the bay. It was always there when she woke up in her ribbon-festooned four poster bed after an afternoon rest.

~

Derick and she had discussed the situation and she knew what she would do. On her last day in Pau, Barbara Waterfield swallowed far more than her usual quantity of sedative. Bad news had arrived. France had surrendered to Germany. The Armistice had been signed on the evening of the 22nd June and the entire Atlantic coastal area, stretching up to Paris and the area further north possibly clearer would come under German control from the 25th. It hadn't been a mistake to leave Menton; it was already occupied by Italian troops, some of whom were living in Le Clos. Once he had checked his beloved wife was fully unconscious, Derick took out an automatic pistol and with one shot, ensured she would never rouse from her stupor. He then turned the gun on himself.

~

Quite apart from the horror of learning their parents were dead, and the fact that they had taken their own lives, it seemed impossible for Humphrey and Tony to believe they were capable of planning such a thing. Their dear rational, erudite, clever, kind-hearted father, who had enjoyed playing the piano in Nancy's house when he had come to stay, relished long days gardening with Humphrey at Hill Pasture, his hands thick with Broxted clay, was gone. And their poor, strange, gentle mother. A woman trapped in another era, traumatised by grief as a young mother, and over subsequent years, diminished by anxiety, would have been impossible to persuade onto a boat for the safety of England. It was such a violent mutual decision for them to have reached. If it was of any consolation at all, it was clear they had made their decision calmly and deliberately. Derick wanted his children to know exactly where their belongings had been stored, jewellery kept safe and gave clear instructions for their recovery after the war ended. His affectionate, long letter continued,

'As I said in my last we gave the Comptoir here cheques for £1100 between us, which ought to last some time, even with a possibility of soaring of prices, at present stable.

I think you should write off everything that was at the Clos as a total loss, but I repeat details about it:

1 About a sixth or a quarter of stuff is left in the Clos, half a dozen things out of most of the rooms.

2 A vanful of the very best is at Tours, which was heavily bombarded yesterday. Hibon, 2 bis rue Marceau, Tours. [Some] Difficulty that he claimed insurance which I had refused saying as instructed by Hocquard, my firend in the rue de la Republique, Menton, that it was already insured. Months later, last month Hibon sent in a bill for storing and insurance. He said he must have insurance or wouldn't continue storing. I replied, very well, let me know again how much that was (300 Fr odd), and send me the receipt of the 800 storage, paid you, by cheque of 20th May. He has not replied.

3 Two vanfuls and what we brought and got over at times, silver among other things, some good pictures, are here, in house or small garage.

4 Two bits of Cat's jewels, nominally £400 are still at Menton in the Comptoir National safe. I sent them the key last week and told them to send the jewels here at their discretion. They say it isn't the right key, and they are at Antibes, and the safe is at Menton. I know it is the right key, and they promised last year if evacuated to send all the safes to Montpelier. That is that, I haven't had the heart to do anything.

Oh by the way, if we went under, the French (or German) Government would lock up our effects, probably the Cogombles or Lafittes would have to show which things were ours and which theirs. Cogombles being on GHQ, the best person to write to would be his mother

Madame Lafitte

25 Plae du Sablar
Dax Dandes

They are merchants there "matieres resineuses" and live between that and the Chateau Bielle, Basses-Pyrenees.

The little safe at the Clos has a key in my old bureau, now in the salon here. I will label it. The key-word is Cham (set so for Chamberlain after Munich), it went wrong and was re-set from "Tony" the old word.

Furniture at Brum as you know, Morris car at Windsor, Maxwell's garage, I am about 6 weeks late with payments. It might be sellable after the war (if the war can be drawn or won).

The Burstalls (who haven't any money here) and the Hamilton Deans who are refuging with us, when their hotel closed on them, have gone down town to see the possibility of escaping to England, via Spain or Portugal. We, nous autres, haven't the heart to do a refugee journey. Whether we may panic at the last moment and try to bolt remains to be seen. I could live in a totally different scene, Canada for instance, but Cat is too frail for that journey. I don't know how to begin it even.

Later. The Vice-Consul told the Knights that the boat was sailing tonight, and told everyone else that there was nothing to be done. The Knights have taken a taxi to Bordeaux, saying that the boat is sure not to sail till morning, he being an old naval man will probably push into it if anyone does, and they are prepared to sleep on the beach, Bordeaux being full like everyone else. The Deans giving up [on] immediate departure have gone away to Lourdes to look after old friends, whom they had left. So we are left with old Madame Mery, who whines and her dog who also whines, and Miriam, who at least is interesting, but in the depths like everyone else. She is a R.C.

I hear Lloyd's Bank is shut, perhaps others, am wondering whether Lloyd's Rugeley will be allowed to send so big a cheque. In that case we shall be reduced to charity.

I bought Knight's automatic, it may be useful if a starving crow or stray tough tried to raid us (at present there seems no sign of crime in France), and always there is fear of [a] concentration camp, but I am hopeful about this.
Bless you dears'

Humphrey was allowed a week's leave. He didn't know what to think any more. Perhaps he should sign up to the army properly if the threat was so real? Was his association with the FAU idealistic to the point of blindness? Nancy and Humphrey paced all day in Kew Gardens together, he trying to thrash it out for himself, she, trying not to influence him. It was a blindingly lovely time of year, and they were in a blindingly lovely place, but now he felt conflicted. If this was the effect of war, shouldn't he fight for freedom? But he knew he couldn't. He resolved to continue as he had all along. He had to remain true to himself and his convictions.

~

The Waterfield double suicide didn't only horrify family members and friends, their servants and household staff were also devastated. Betty Duff, the one-time governess to Humphrey and Tony as young boys, but latterly housekeeper and companion to Barbara was especially distraught. When the news of the occupation of France came through, she bade her employers farewell and with their blessing, fled for England on a ship from Bayonne. She arrived in Plymouth and made her way to Scotland. From a quiet suburban road in Aberdeen, she penned a letter to a friend on the 27th August 1940:

'My dear Audrey
Yes. Wasn't it an awful catastrophe? Barbara had decided long ago that if the worst came to the worst (Germans conquering France) she would just sleep away. She was desperately afraid of what might happen. She vowed never to try and make a "get away" with the

crowd. She felt she would never survive such a thing. I myself don't think she would. She had a horror of a German concentration camp, much for Derick as for herself and her idea of an English winter for Derick was also a nightmare. So, she took an easy way out. Derick was terribly depressed about the war and almost more so about the peace. He often said the world would not be fit to live in. If I had stayed on, I should probably have done as they did – but I did not see how I could so came away with two friends – I left on a Thursday and the following Monday or Tuesday during the night, the awful deed took place. B took an over-dose and Derick shot himself. I had a heart-rending letter from Emma. She and Victoire found them on Tuesday morning, 25th June. I had compared with an easy journey in a Dutch boat from Bayonne to Plymouth. Only 24 hours en route, though 4 nights sitting up in our clothes. Poor Humphrey and Tony refused to believe the calamity and still can't understand what brought them to hasten the event. You know Barbara could never motor any distance, so getting to the Spanish frontier for was for her impossible (it was closed at that time anyhow). Physical discomfort was almost intolerable. So, what was left. Humphrey is working in a hospital in Gloucester with the Friends Ambulance Unit. I believe they are very badly housed. This is no country to be in. It is not pleasant. How I dread the winter here 24 years since I have experienced one. There has been no warm weather since I got back. They had it all before I came. I can't imagine my life away from the Waterfields. I feel it has quite come to an end and nothing seems to matter. I am quite numb.

Yours with love, Betty Duff

CHAPTER TWENTY-ONE

War Garden

1940-41

*'Very occasionally he got weekend leave and we would spend
it as ever planning and planting at Broxted.'*

The following months left Humphrey bereaved and disorientated. For a few days he remained in Essex with Nancy, at Orford, visiting Hill Pasture, working in the garden, trying to paint and having terrible, disturbing dreams. Letters from France began to trickle through, and the more they read, the more resolved the Waterfield's suicide plan had appeared to be. It turned out that Betty Duff had originally been part of a suicide pact. She had planned to end it all by "taking an overdose of Vernol" with Barbara. In his final letter to his children dated the 24th June, Derick began, *'My dear Babies'*, he expressed his concern for the welfare of the servants after his and Barbara's deaths, and instructed their sons to ensure they were provided for, along with the adored Betty. Derick knew that when they eventually did kill themselves, the aftermath would not be straightforward, *'suicide is easy in a civilised country with sympathetic officials: in the agony of people it is less convenient,'* he wrote. His very last words to his sons were *'Goodbye darlings – be good men – Pop.'* And that was that. The final, precious, posthumous point of contact.

The war worsened. Hermann Göring, the Nazi egomaniac in white satin 'with a bosom full of medals' observed by Nancy at the pre-war Berlin dinner party, was in full military flow. On the 2nd August 1940 he issued his 'Eagle Day' directive: a plan to destroy Britain by air. On the seventh of 7th September 1940, on a sunny afternoon, the London Blitz began. *The first night the London docks were bombed was unforgettable: the sky turned a bright flowing red, while the guns banged and boomed'* observed Nancy.

Humphrey returned to Gloucester to hospital work and continued through the summer and autumn. Knowing that Nancy was taking care of the garden, her prose painting pictures of its beauty in her letters, was some sort of consolation. The practicalities of the day-to-day running of the place now fell to her. She kept him abreast of the garden triumphs and its financial outgoings. She could collect some rent for him if she managed to organise a tenant, and that would help cover some running costs. Amongst the dull toil of Gloucester hospital work with the Quakers, letters about the garden were like a window onto a brighter world. The plants in the garden seemed to take on personalities, and the pair discussed them like human characters. While bombs fell from the sky, and the world lacked certainty, the garden provided them with an unspoilt and innocent corner in which to retreat.

'My dear one, I feel so vexed I was just starting out for a lovely long day at Broccers and was going to write my letter there when the blasted siren went and the usual hordes appeared in the sky. It becomes a trifle boring – three goes yesterday and two every other day but despite all the alarms nothing really alarming save one crash yesterday which made the house rock – perhaps only an anti-aircraft gun but I can't think where from. It's not good for the

children . . . dear Funny [Nancy's nickname for Humphrey] *I wish you were here it's all so still and lovely – the magic gone up to a point because everything is so dried up but the pleasure of its being empty is enough in itself.* Mutabilis *is almost the loveliest thing; some of the flowers a pale creamy yellow, the others brilliant rosy pink. I have just had lunch and am sitting with very little on indeed so do hope there won't be many callers. I have been trying to get the house back to something like normality. Mr C was here on Friday and we moved all the furniture then there are lots of odds and ends. Mrs Wareham is being very kind and comes in to clean, I don't know if the paint will ever recover without another repaint but it's useless to do anything drastic so long as the military may return or bombs descend . . . Mr Reynolds, like me is longing for your hols. I wish you could have got away this week when we still have the house but that would be too much to hope for. Shall you be able to catch the 4.30 train on the 12th and get to London that evening – it would make such a lot of difference – do try – it was lovely to get your long letter on Friday and hear you had captured a Mozartian moment. I've had some rather good, but more Virginia Woolfian moments. Something to do I think with being physically very tired – the top layer of one's mind shuts off and one is left with a sudden strange intensity of vision and feeling and shape of a magnolia leaf, or a rose on the dining room table suddenly seems absolute and all one's doings and surroundings simply aren't there at all. I am just as pleased to be having to work so hard at the Centre even though all I do is menial and filthy – chiefly washing jam jars from the dump – it makes the time pass quick (sic) and one is far too occupied to be worried or afraid. The air is suddenly full of hums again – too high for one to see them – luckily one cannot hear the sirens here so can go quietly about one's business – my business is to love the* cistus *bed and if I am troubled in the process, please remember how happy I've been at Broccers. XXN*

My funny dear I can hardly bear this heavenly Broxted weather either; it all seems a waste . . . dear one I suppose you couldn't get away this week – no I know you can't – and it's just silly to think about it But I do miss you when everything is so enchantingly beautiful.'

Nancy's fleeting mention of the Centre was a reference to a colossal national food provision effort. Now that war had been declared, the NFWI was a ready-made network of thousands of women; women who could be trusted with the precious hoards of rationed sugar the government was about to hand over to them. The NFWI had already been utilised to great effect for the evacuee programme, with thousands of urban children moving from cities to country homes, living with members of the Institutes. Now the members could help feed the nation with vitamin packed fruit jam. Ugley village hall was no longer simply a meeting place for local women to gather, exchange ideas and sing. The memorial hall built by William Tennant, like hundreds of centres up and down the country, had become a jam production centre. Today's faintly derisory association of the Women's Institute with jam-making originated from this highly responsible task given to them during the war.

It had been a good summer for fruit in 1940. Plums had been particularly prolific. By today's standards, the idea of sugar loaded jam being a healthy source of vitamins seems terrifying, but with limited fresh produce, jam was the best way of storing the nation's fruit and preserving food for national consumption. In 1940, there were 2,600, NFWI jam production centres, many in village halls, the following year were 4,500. Anyone who had a surplus of fruit in their garden could sell it at a Centre. *'What began as a WI Produce Guild project in 1940 became a government-sponsored, nationwide effort of women everywhere'* reported the WI committee.

'I was inspecting, I had to check on cleanliness, on packaging, on labelling, and . . . sugar content too. The reason we were checking the

sugar was that we were given sugar on trust. There was utter and complete honesty, but it was a temptation to syphon away sugar and use it for yourself during those days of high rationing.' recalled a WI member, Viola Williams, in the book *Village Voices*. At the end of the year the Minister of Food, Lord Woolton declared the work had been a "fine example of democratic action" and "of national importance, demanding administrative ability of a high order at the Headquarters of your organisation."

In her letters to Humphrey, throughout the war, Nancy consistently underplayed her role, dropping in the occasional mention of her activities and responsibilities. Her focus for him, was Hill Pasture. She was, in reality, doing far more than washing jam jars in the village hall and thinking about the weather and 'Broccers.' In 1939, the formidable Chairman, Lady Denman, became head of the Womens' Land Army. In 1940, her Vice-Chairman, the academic and popular Grace Haddow, died of pneumonia. Nancy was promoted into the vacant position and became a co-Vice Chairman. It was a position of national responsibility. *'It made such a change in my life. I felt ill prepared to be her successor. It was all the more daunting because I knew Lady Denman had little confidence in my capacities. It meant even more travelling; I could no longer concentrate on the music as we were responsible for everything that went on all over the country. I wish I had kept a record of the places I stayed in – sometimes in a council house, sometimes at Althorp, sometimes in a Welsh farm (no plumbing), sometimes with the Devonshires. It was a good way to learn to be elastic about the company one kept,'* wrote Nancy. Unlike her brother Ernest who had tried to influence international diplomacy and politics with ultimately no tangible or positive outcome, Nancy was rising to a position of practical responsibility that would affect the entire country for the better. Nancy was doing far more than simply weeding flower beds for the love of her life.

After the fall of France, French soldiers had begun to escape into England, where De Gaulle's Free French Resistance Force began to assemble. The call went out for anyone bilingual in French who could help. Humphrey with his perfect French, was promptly moved from Gloucester to Surrey to train in Camberley with the newly formed Hadfield Spears Unit. This was an Anglo-French volunteer medical unit which served initially with the 4th French army in Lorraine, eastern France, during the Second World War from February 1940, until it was forced to retreat on 9th June ahead of the German advance. Its official French designation at that time was Ambulance Chirurgical Légère de Corps d'Armée 282. The unit made its way across France via Bordeaux to Arcachon, from where it was evacuated back to Britain, arriving at Plymouth on 26th June. The unit re-grouped and re-equipped in Britain, adding several members of the FAU (Humphrey included) to its ranks, and prepared to ship out once more, this time to the Middle East.

The Hadfield Spears Unit operated along similar principles to the Scandinavian FAU convoy. As mainly Quakers and all pacifists, their mission was to provide medical back up to whichever military force happened to be in the field, in this case the Free French (1st Free French Forces). They would journey out to the Middle East, via South Africa, setting up and operating mobile field hospitals, erecting vast tents, housing mobile wards and operating theatres. Humphrey's unit comprised of women drivers, nurses, doctors, mechanics and like Humphrey, men trained as ward orderlies, drivers and general logistical backup. His friend and Arabic speaking Quaker neighbour, Nik Alderson, was leading the mission. Familiar faces as well as new would serve with the Hadfield Spears including Humphrey's musical co-driver from the Scandinavian mission, Stephen Verney. Others included Frederick, 'Freddy' Temple and piano loving John Hamilton Mills, known as 'Hammy.' "We were an extraordinary mixture of academics and practical people, a very strange amalgam' recalled Freddy Temple, "women drivers of the upper class, the French doctors who had come out from France, then a marvellous group of nurses."

While he trained at Camberley, for the moment, Nancy and

Humphrey were relatively near each other and continued with their garden planting plan. Chatsworth, the glorious primal spine of the garden was growing well, but needed, in Humphrey's opinion, more yew. '*We spent our days gardening and our evenings playing Bach and Mozart (especially The Flute) on my EMG with its enormous horn*' wrote Nancy. But on Thursday, 20th March 1941, Humphrey and Nancy stood facing each other outside London's Middlesex Hospital and shared a final "bleak" goodbye. They had no real sense of when, or if, they would see each other again. He really couldn't miss his train this time. At two thirty in the afternoon, Humphrey boarded the troop train at Kings Cross, bound for Glasgow. It was, in a curious way, an easier parting for Humphrey. He had been used to the division of life for as long as he could remember. Holidays in one place, another part of life in another. A hug and kiss from the woman he loved most, once his mother, sometimes his Great Aunt Meta, and now Nancy, the nearest thing he had to a wife or sweetheart, and off he went, apparently accepting what was required of him.

Yet he was never going to head off to war with his jaw clenched and emotion stifled. His inner thoughts skipped from the profound to the irreverent and superficial. As he entered the Officers' Mess for his final London meal, he was struck by the gaiety of the arrangement, '*the mess looked inviting, pretty little tablecloths with red and white napkins: it might have been a small French restaurant.*' The journey was also convivial. 'Hammy' helped '*lug his heavy suitcase*' for him: Nik invited him to the first-class cabin for dinner. They arrived at dawn and waited in the grey cold of a Glasgow morning for four hours. Finally, hundreds of troops, commanding officers, staff and the FAU members poured onto the ship, bound for the Atlantic Ocean and Africa.

Once on board, there was initial confusion about which army rank the rankless Quakers would 'mess' with. As far as their education and backgrounds went, they were comparable to officers, but the luxuries enjoyed by the officers didn't correlate with the plain living, high thinking Quaker approach. '*We finally exchanged the damask of the Warrant Officers for the Corinthian bagatelle boards of the sergeants. A 5-course breakfast in the WO's, although the puritan might frown, the inner man made the best of. And though demoted in the mess we kept our cabins. I was lucky enough to have one to myself. A great joy was the porthole just above the bed. Nothing could be nicer than to lie listening to the noise of the sea; a sea wind blowing about one's ears*' explained Humphrey.

Although he felt companionable and intellectually comfortable with the men in his immediate circle and unit, Humphrey was otherwise reserved and avoided conversation with soldiers. '*Personally, I feel stunned by this heaving mass of khaki and have hardly spoken two words to anyone on board. Put them in civilian clothes, break them up into manageable units, I could battle with their lives and loves, as it is, my natural shyness and detachment prevail over my humanity and I am too lazy to make the effort that comes more easily to the more human Ham and Hugh, to say nothing of Arnold and Harry, Charles and Dennis. One must I think accept one's limitations: my ivory tower though open to all, is approached in single file.*'

Humphrey found much to enjoy in the strange new life. He was free to learn and ponder for the seven weeks of the voyage, '*I could go on for ever in this intelligent idleness reading my 50 lines of Sophocles, doing Italian with Hammy & Nik, modern Greek with Ian, chess with Hammy, talk with everybody walking the deck, watching Orion all end ways, the Plough standing up his head, sinking, as the days draw in & thicken, into a warm inactive sweat.*'

Of course, Humphrey knew he was at war, but his immersion into the reality in which he found himself was only partial. Part engaged, part entirely absent, his thoughts drifted from the immediate to the tangential. '*On the Friday we got the news that Benghazi had been retaken by the Italians, and what was of much greater importance to some of us, that Virginia Woolf had died. I feel she had written all she had to say but you never can tell. A fitting end when you come to think of it. In 'Roger Fry' she had written the swan song of her Bloomsbury civilisation. Alas it was mine too, in a way.'* For an intellectual and romantic, it was a pleasure to discover there were 'some of us' who felt the same way as he did on board.

CHAPTER TWENTY-TWO

Heat and Dust

1941

'I reason that this garden of ours in something we have made together and it's got a sort of precious quality almost as a child might have.'

The *Riena del Pacifico*, once used as a grand ocean liner, taking passengers across the Atlantic from Liverpool to South America via Bermuda was now Humphrey's troop ship. There was no chance of approaching Suez via the Mediterranean, carving forty days at sea from the former old ocean route: Fascist Italian forces would prevent it. The long, pre-Suez Canal journey, skirting the Cape of Good Hope, and up from the south, past the Horn of Africa was their itinerary. They passed the Azores on the 29th March and powered south towards Freetown on the coast of West Africa. The Sierra Leone capital had been transformed into an Allied naval and military hub for the duration of the war. Thousands of Allied forces passed through it, refuelling, restocking and allowing themselves some respite from the swell of the ocean.

The ship anchored on the 5th April in the West African harbour but no passengers were allowed to leave the ship, nor were they allowed to buy any fruit from the locals in the small boats that bobbed in the surrounding marine waters, plying their wares. '*We lay four days and sweated,*' wrote Humphrey, '*boatfuls of natives began to come alongside, their dark hair and faces a centre in a sea of green banana. Watermelons in the bows, what could be more delicious? But the edict had gone out that no-one was to buy from boats so we had no option but to ignore the blandishments – they seemed to be utterly vulgarised, could talk knowingly of London and Liverpool and their songs, such as the 'Lambeth Walk'. How vile a thing is Imperialism!*'

By the morning of 19th April, the ship reached Durban and finally they were allowed to disembark. Humphrey thought it looked like the South of France. '*On first impression from the sea, rather like Nice. About the same size, the same shapes of buildings what look like pine-covered hills and on the sky-line cypresses.*' Four days of rest and relaxation in Durban took many forms. Some of the men dined with their local hosts, or explored the surrounding countryside. Others sought out women and bars but Humphrey was most content to lose himself in the exotic and alien flora of the Durban Botanic Gardens. '*I spent the afternoon very happily in the Botanic Gardens alone. It was a pleasure to be alone, a pleasure to wander through the peace of the garden, to listen to the cicadas and the strange bird noises, to look up into the intricate luxuriance of the leaves. It was hot and the sun filtered pleasantly down through the green parasols onto the brightly coloured things below. The labelling was poor and the garden lacked the plants I sought for, but I succeeded in tracing the foliage plant one saw everywhere Acalpha Tricolor from the New Hebrides, a plant whose leaves varied from a bright claret colour to olive green and a greenish lemon. I talked a little to a charming gardener who told me the name of Torenia and Solanum Wendlandii, Solanum W was an exquisitely vital thing with curly leaves rather like an opened peapod . . . There was a beautiful Ipomoea with flowers like Burgundy, the buds balls of almost black and 4 leaves in a cluster, a little like one of the more exotic horse chestnuts. I drew them all and listened to the musical language of the Zulus indolently weeding in the sun – others potting up under a spreading ficus [weeping fig], their bodies black upon the brilliant earth. But it was time to go back . . . and reluctantly I retraced my steps among the lily pools along the hedge of cactus with the scarlet two petalled flower to the gate . . .'*

On the 23rd April, the ship departed from Durban, and Humphrey took comfort in the thought that *'the convoy began to move off and we could see in other ships the sight we must ourselves have presented, decks lined with cheering figures, docks with fluttering handkerchiefs from a thousand girls. The halcyon days are over, before us lies the Red Sea, the heat and the beastliness, behind us at least the consolation that at any rate in one happy corner of the globe life is still lived in light and not in darkness, in peace and in prosperity.'*

On 1st May, Humphrey's ship entered the Gulf of Aden and on the evening of 9th May it arrived in Suez and the men disembarked. From now, and for an unknown length of time, Humphrey and his Unit would live and work in what would become known as The Middle East Theatre of War.

Like an amorphous, continually evolving organism, awash with incompatible bacteria competing for dominance, the territory in which the Hadfield Spears Unit would travel, ebbed and flowed in strategic significance throughout the Second World War. Battle after battle, fight after fight, the countries and ancient kingdoms that Europeans had held as colonies and protectorates, had transformed into a bloody zone of conflict that spared no section of society. The Axis Powers and Allied Powers would fight over land they considered theirs and depended on for global dominance. Desert communities, local rulers eyeing independence, kings (like the pro-German Shah of Persia replaced by his pro-Britsh son), citizens of ancient seats of power and religion, were all dragged into the conflict. Nowhere was safe or sacred. Success in the area, could trigger invasions deep into Asia and Africa.

De Gaulle's Free French army, pitched against their fellow

countrymen and pro-Hitler Vichy French troops, fought for dominance over former French colonies, such as Syria and Lebanon. They would kill, maim, and defeat each other, then move onto the next push for territory. Beyond the two main adversaries, national opportunities were eyed. Mussolini, in his loyalty to the 'Axis', would attempt invasions to expand existing Italian colonies like Libya, and attack Egypt, Tunisia and Palestine. Suspected plans to supply weapons or troops to arm the next invasion, wherever it might be, would be dashed or realised by battles fought over strategic ground. And just when it might seem that progress in one direction or another was being made, tactics would change under brilliant new military strategists like Germany's 'Desert Fox', Field Marshal Rommel, or British Field Marshal 'Monty' Montgomery and previous gains would be lost and new battlelines drawn.

All of this required medical back up. Wherever the war raged, surgeons, ward orderlies, mechanics, drivers, nurses would be required. The Hadfield Spears supporting the Free French would locate themselves near the battle zones. Sometimes they would pitch a field hospital on what appeared to be the middle of nowhere at all, on, as one member of the FAU described, 'a patch of sand', other times, they would find themselves in an empty, purpose-built hospital in a recently conquered town, with all the convenience of tiled floors, wards for patients and running water.

This 'Middle East Theatre of War' stretched from North Africa to the Holy Lands and beyond. Colonial rule from Italy, Britain and France had masked local power struggles and yearnings for independence for decades. Conflict during the Second World War didn't just bring a superficial scarring to the external appearance of nations or groups of people who considered themselves alike. Conflict liberated disorder and from that flowed opportunity from deep within. Existing rulers and regimes could be overthrown, jihad could be declared, national identities switched and names of countries redrawn, altered and created.

The 'Spears' as they became known, began their expedition in Sarafand, packed their equipment, and set out across the Sinai Desert. The heat was unlike anything Humphrey and most of his companions had ever known before. Dry, merciless desert heat, leaving sand in the mouth, teeth grinding involuntarily on minute grains. Any water exposed to the air evaporated instantly. Their enormous water tankers warmed to such a temperature that the drinking water boiled. Driving was difficult too. '*The hot wind blew off the desert, the heat burnt one's arms and eyes. I wondered that first hour if I could keep my eyes open if I were driving. The second period I took over, the worst was when a wind blew up the sand and it whipped one's face. The heat came in curious patches, as if some fiend were amusing himself with a pair of bellows.*' recorded Humphrey. At times the journey seemed interminable, '*the desert went on and on, occasionally a few goats or camels browsed the spiky grey bushlets . . . all along the tarmac road the empty drums lay rejected, together with spare cans of petrol which had been emptied and thrown away. The landscape was one vast natural and human scrap heap. A few goats or camels grazed and hobbled, in the charge of Arab women or boys. At last heavenly deliverance, we arrived at a frontier post. A great earthenware jar of cool water was emptied in a quarter of an hour. I had been drinking water from the water tanks, hot and rusty . . . oh the coolness of that water in an enamelled mug after the metal water bottles!*' They journeyed on to Beersheba where a shower, supper and beer awaited them in the coolness of a modern, concrete courtyard. In spite of the fatigue, heat and dust, he was still able to look at his surroundings with an artist's eye: '*lovely colour, piles of oranges in the sun, bright cottons against dark, sometimes vaulted shops. Nothing one wanted to possess, much to paint.*'

By mid-May, the Spears had become fully operational desert workers: pitching tents in burning heat and adapting to the merciless environment. They would arrive, load and unload lorries, pitch tents, attend to patients and move on again. They learnt the ways of the desert early on. Humphrey and his companions succumbed to the temptation to strip off their shirts only once. Sunburnt to an agonising level, their scarlet legs and torsos were rendered even more painful by the thorns of desert thistles irritating their skin further as they walked about. The sand floors of their tents swarmed with biting ants. Discomfort increased irritation and resentment. Humphrey observed that *'morale not improved by learning that an Arab cook has been engaged for the officers and women who continue in their huts with oleander and bougainvillea at the door. Americans sink in our estimation by their idleness . . . jackals and hyenas heard at night. Hope we have settled ants by petrol poured down their nests. My unpleasant job, involving sucking petrol into a tube for siphon, breakfast and lunch taste of petrol and nasty petrol at that.'*

Although the work in the first weeks was physically demanding, the main hardship was that it was repetitive and dull, yet his solace was in beauty where he could find it. Humphrey greatly admired the architecture, mosaics and colours that surrounded them and the sound of the wind in the trees reminded him of the South of France. *'Lovely to lie listening to the wind in the eucalyptus outside, full of the overtones of other winds in other trees [like the] Mistral or Sirocco. One of the consolations of growing old must be the overtones in all experience till at the last perhaps they overweigh it and nothing has a clear outline anymore.'*

Desert life, though far from where he wanted to be, had in the first months at least, these aesthetic consolations. Nancy's reports on the garden gave him an alternative reality to inhabit and escape to. It was a life-line for both of them. Her love for him and the garden gave her something active and tangible to feel and describe, when in reality, he was hundreds of miles away, unseeable and untouchable, possibly forever. Nancy's letters didn't just paint pictures of the garden for him, they gave him hope, and for a fleeting moment, the feeling she was with him. She gave him news of every plant, the shape of the clouds, the shadow of the trees, the frost in the morning and the heat of the English summer sun. She spun tales of their earthly paradise using her own lyrical prose, confident in their shared sense of wonder at the beauty of nature:

'May 18th

My darling Funny one, Summer at last, after snow two days ago, and I write sitting in the porch with the sun beating down and all the birds singing. This new time is such a godsend to the not very early riser for one has all the magic of 6 o'clock over 8 o'clock breakfast. I made up my mind yesterday to leave everything undone and go to Broxted really early. O if only you had been there! The balsam and the sweet briar so strong as almost to seem tangible, the grass still dewy and shining, forget-me-not a solid line of blue against white wall, the willows on the road feathered with green, blue shadows under them and behind the newly ploughed field, like brown corrugated cardboard, and then the birds – there never were so many. Nancy Graham, who was at Crowns for the night came over to visit me and she couldn't get over the birds and the beauty and thought what lovely fun we must have had making it all, indeed we have. I was busy as a bee, mostly mowing but for the intervals of getting my breath I weeded the spartium (Spanish Broom) bed – it was too delicious, warm crumbly earth and the smell of sweet briar. Mr R very busy scything, he really is doing a lot of work now but pray of pray what are we going to do with the grass between the new hedges – 'all owd twitch – can't do nuthin with it'. I am a little worried over Chatsworth, I would dearly like to see it rain. One great excitement dear one, the shrubbery . . . in flower – seven or eight, quite exquisite just our sort of flower – perfect in form and snowy white.'

Humphrey's friend Peter Townsend had visited her; he had been busy in Oxford learning Chinese and was soon to leave on an FAU convoy to China: *'I did so enjoy having Peter here yesterday he looked thin and very grubby but was charming as ever. We lay in the sun then he mowed the bit below the steps: it's a great relief to have that done as I couldn't tackle it myself but shall be able to keep it, [now] the worst of it [is done]. After tea we walked down the valley and through the wood. The larch brilliant above the foreground of pines and bluebells underneath and such smells.'*

Nancy was also saying a long goodbye to her beloved father. William Augustus Tennant was was slowly fading from life at Orford. *'No change here though I think Papa seems rather weaker this morning – he keeps reiterating that he died last week and that we must announce it in the Times. I long for your comfortable presence at this time but on the whole am glad you are out of this strange, sad England, Bless you.'*

CHAPTER TWENTY-THREE

Love and Attraction

1941

'But then there is the problem of you.'

Humphrey was a romantic. Although he declared his 'ivory tower' was 'open to all', from the age of twenty-four, only Nancy occupied the most important position. She was his most beloved. However, there were others who were very beloved too. His interest in his fellow man, regardless of sex or gender was intense and child-like. He admired physical beauty, artistic sensitivity and intelligence and when they were combined in one person, he found it irresistible.

Before the war, Peter Townsend had impressed him deeply. Humphrey had seen traits of his own temperament in Peter, who was sincere, devoted to art and single minded in his determination to pursue his interests. He was convinced Peter was a genius.

Peter's passion for music and the Chinese language had absorbed him from his schooldays and selection for the China Convoy was a dream as far as his interests and linguistic ambitions went. Much as Humphrey might have wanted to join Peter on the Rangoon adventure, his bilingual French was too useful to the Hadfield Spears and so they were destined to go their separate ways. Humphrey appeared to have been childishly sulky about the future of their friendship. Peter, over ten years younger, tried to console him: '*all the last week I have been busy with new sounds & an enhancing field of philosophy and art. But I do not forget you, or your ridiculous idea that we shall meet five years hence and treat each other as strangers. Nor do I think the four years I am pledged to will bring me regret, because the more I read of the Chinese, the more I fall in love with them . . . I think one's duty is to progress . . . & live a few years with people on the unit with whom I shall perhaps be out of sympathy, many a strange race whom I must go out to understand & not expect them to offer themselves in the way of books & plays & music, will be of great value to me. But then there is the problem of you, as I wanted you to hold on to, & you had done me so much good in many ways. What am I to do? Books will prove a poor substitute for someone one really felt responsive. When do you go? If you have any leave or in London over the weekend again, I want to see you once more and can take Saturday and Sunday a fortnight hence would be best for me. Now that I have written all this, I want more & more of Funnyman* [Humphrey's nickname] *Love Peter.*'

In 1940, he had audaciously asked Humphrey for money to pay for music lessons: '*now I have music, & still find it whistling round & round inside me, looking somewhere for an outlet, and I have to hope that you will help me. I want to have 2 or 3 lessons a week & an hour or an hour & a half's practice at Alcott's music shop each day, & have in fact arranged to have my first lesson in aural training tomorrow evening. If I am to do this, I shall have to have £1 per week & I lack the courage to write home for all of this, although it would not be wholly refused. Could I ask you for this, while I am up here, & without trying to pretend that it would be loan! Although I shall not feel bitter or hard if you cannot. I think it is a question of capturing the second dream period and keeping it developing its creative energy & somehow I shall do it. How fantastic this feeling seems after so long a time of intolerable diffidence!'*

Peter was clever to turn to Humphrey for support in his intellectual and musical ambitions because he knew Humphrey understood such single-minded enthusiasm. Just as the teenaged Humphrey had been obsessive in his desire to learn Italian and study Dante independently at school, Peter was in love with Mandarin. Their worlds intertwined beyond the FAU too, as William, Peter's brother, was an artist and a Professor of Art at the Slade.

But in the spring and early summer of 1941, Peter, although much missed, was not with him and Humphrey was enchanted by someone else. From the moment he had set off for the Middle East, a young man had captured his attention, to the point of what appeared to be teenage infatuation on Humphrey's part.

~

Hamilton Mills, known as 'Hammy' was the new object of Humphrey's affection. He admired Hammy's musical ability; he was an excellent pianist, yet Humphrey felt Hammy's youthful vigour and uncomplicated cheerfulness masked something more profound which piqued his interest. Just as he revelled in the variety of flowers and plants in the Durban Botanic Gardens, so Hammy was a specimen for Humphrey to admire and analyse. The friendship began before the ship had even sailed. Hammy had helped him with his suitcase on the journey to the ship, a gesture of kindness and attention that Humphrey thought worth recording in his diary. For a time, he filled his diary pages with thoughts and tales of adventures with Hammy.

'*Stood on deck till midnight with Hammy talking. Both oblivious of the lapse of time. Pro and con the machine age, pro and con the BBC, each time more emphatic over the second, in which he agreed least. A lovely night though the stars are more beautiful, rare jewels at sundown, that the too-rich galaxy of night. I am bad at human beings because I can only be interested in one or two at a time. I concentrate all my attention on Hammy in a ridiculous way when the boat must be full of interesting people. I am pretty constant too, and only change my friends when accident compels it, so that at the present rate I shall have known only a dozen or so persons really well in an existence even if prolonged to three score and ten.'* He also found Hammy physically beautiful. *'Found Hammy almost naked on the bed and drew him. When he awoke he took off his pants. Astonishing how the figure came together. Naked the forms take up a rhythmic sequence and the whole construction takes on a divine beauty. Amazing that so beautiful a thing should disappear a minute later into a mess of ill-fitting khaki.'* He obsessively analysed Hammy's face, trying to elucidate some deeper understanding of this person who had caught his attention. Could he, like Humphrey, be a true artist?

'. . . The eyes, the way the pretty way the hair, straight and black and very fine, hangs over the neat, rounded forehead, the good nose – now ugly, rather 'chetif', the funny triangular face, the small chin, the mouth drawn into ugly snarls at the corners – a pose mostly but founded on fact perhaps, or is it that most dangerous thing a pose . . . Hammy is direct, forceful, never hesitates . . . perhaps he really is an all-round man, too well balanced to be an artist, too much character, too far from Keats' passive existence, having an independent existence, flowing through all things.'

Hammy may have been gloriously good-looking from top to toe, but Humphrey himself was very handsome too. His FAU registration card reveals a classically good-looking man with a quizzical expression and slight smile dancing across his lips. FAU friends wrote to Nancy mid-war describing his "well-knit trunk" concealed in a towel, about which she quoted back to Humphrey in a letter to him, saying teasingly that she wished she could see the same view herself. Now aged thirty-six he was in the prime of life. Women and men adored him, and, in those days, people thought little of admiring each other physically, with no real suggestions of furtive sexual longing or conquest, legal or otherwise.

In September 1941, Peter wrote two final letters to his friend before setting sail for China.

'Dear Humphrey

The penultimate letter. News has come more suddenly than we imagined or wished, of a boat, and we shall leave in a very few days. The next 48 hours will be spent in trains & buses & rapid glances at people and places. I had very much hoped to see Nancy and Broxted – but it is too impossible. Instead, I have to wrestle with the unhappiness of leaving, and of finding oneself the incomprehending centre of so much affection. Blessed are they that receive. How much more difficult it is, and hopeless. Now for the trains and buses and rapid glances, and later the terrible tiredness. Love Peter.'

And then, in Glasgow, sitting in his room at the Regent Hotel before his ship sailed the following morning, Peter wrote again. He knew Humphrey had his painting and a life with Nancy to look forward to after the war. Or at least that seemed to be Peter's way of signing off their friendship for the foreseeable future.

'Dear Humphrey

Half past one in the morning only a few hours before sailing and two years in China [is] neither here nor there. I am very indifferent to time and place, and only wish others were. I had a few words with Nancy over the telephone last night, and heard that you were contented and, most important, painting. Sometimes I have envied you since you left, sometimes not, but I look forward to your settling down in Broxted more than all else. I value the two years in the FAU if only for that tragi-comic ham side in Birmingham, and all it led up to. Preserve me from sentimentality! The next few hours must be dedicated to sleep, and after that a day that requires no thought or initiative. Sometime, I shall plant with my own hand the cream (bad word, but tired) of Chinese flora in Essex soil.

My love, Peter'

Peter remained in China for years. He would eventually become an expert on Chinese language, society and art. In the late 1940s he met an American communist journalist, Rose Yarmudian, and married her, returning to Europe in 1949 when life in Communist China became restrictive.

Humphrey didn't receive the farewell letters from Peter until late 1941, possibly early 1942 and by that stage, he and Hammy had enjoyed time off from ambulance work together. In his diaries he wrote about the experiences like one half of a love-struck honey-mooning couple. He described the dawn after a night sleeping the under the stars: '*The sunset was staggering: a great theatrical sky . . . the stars were shining in a sky that had cleaved . . . waking was exquisite: the unfinished walls framed in the grey concrete bricks the sun turned to a golden yellow, a washed pearly sky, the palest of pale blue like a tempura painting . . .*

～

Then, as with so many infatuations and first flushes of interest, something changed. After a few months, Hammy began to distance himself from Humphrey, leaving the latter feeling confused, rejected and hurt. Humphrey reacted petulantly, regressing to the same childish behaviour he had displayed with Peter Townsend. He imbued the slackening friendship with hyperbolic significance, invoking William Blake's cynicism in his *Clod and Pebble* poem, of the true nature of 'love' and its propensity to build a hell in what had been love's heaven. He found Hammy's friendships with other men hard to accept: '*sad that I should have seen my friendship with Hammy as me the clod and he the pebble. Humiliating and bitter to think that I put more weight on it that it would bear. Now he has gone off with Stephen I am left lonely in a crowd – almost unpleasant – they have more in common of course – age and music . . . [but] . . . it was Hammy who sought me out at Camberley when Hugh was my only friend in this party . . .*'

～

He likened his hurt to the retracted tentacles of a sensitive sea anemone. The truth was that in spite of academic ability, artistic talent and physical maturity, Humphrey was emotionally childlike. He was unable and didn't want to behave in an adult way. His obliviousness to the effect he had had on Nancy in the early days of their friendship was infantile in its obtuseness. His petulant sulking, when people disappointed him, even though he kept it to himself, and couched it in sophisticated literary thinking, lacked empathy. He was very aware of this, as he wrote in his diary he felt like a small boy of about six, less emotionally mature than the men in his unit, most of whom were a decade younger than him. Humphrey was still in his head, the young fictitious John of his short story, *'The Trees'*, who decided that after his sixth birthday, *'the best of his life was over.'* Once he had recovered from the humiliation of Hammy 'going off' with Stephen, he consoled himself with the assurance of his friendship with Nancy and Peter. *'I only care for people with a certain subtlety of mind,* he declared, *"I miss Nancy, I miss Peter. Hammy is a borderline case.'* Peter was miles away, on the other side of the world, but Nancy was a constant loving presence through her innumerable letters. Her support had meant his life had moved in a direction that brought him profound happiness. *'One cannot think of anyone in the Unit except perhaps myself, who have Nancy, my garden and my painting to make me want to live, who would be more willing to die.'* Nancy's role in keeping Humphrey's spirits from entirely failing would become increasingly critical. Only she could keep Hill Pasture alive in his head.

CHAPTER TWENTY-FOUR

Grim Realities

1941

'All Syria is not worth the screams of one amputated man. I read Plato to keep sane. I hope in my next existence I may be a plant. The mind seeks an escape unconsciously. A joint of meat on the bed screams and screams even under morphine.'

In early June 1941, while the Battle of Damascus raged, the Hadfield Spears arrived at Deraa sixty-three miles south of the city. It was a miserable place, of flies, filth and the stench of corpses. Hospital work became more intense with injured Free French soldiers arriving daily. Troops groaned waiting for medical attention on stretchers, some with shattered limbs requiring amputation, others with terrible facial disfigurements. The hospital staff bickered in their fatigue, with gunfire in the distance.

'*We have a heartrending job,*' wrote Humphrey, ' *– the theatre – I went to help one night – is a ghoulish affair, one surgeon is good, one bad. Anaesthetists at first very unsuccessful, amid screams, one man, after an unsuccessful local anaesthetic had most of his buttock removed. The* man I saw being operated on was blinded in both eyes. Hammy had a case: they undid the dressing, a finger dropped off. The French nurses fight with the English. I was alone in the hospital last night, supper time 7 o'clock, the first machine gunning. De Gaulle paid us a visit yesterday: professional and calm. This is just what I objected to about this expedition and Nik assured me would not happen, we are being used in a doubtful filibuster against Vichy.' So many Free French soldiers died, the unit fashioned make-shift wooden crosses from disused fruit boxes.

Nancy's replies were a blinding flash of beauty and a reminder of his earthly paradise 'My darling Funny, whenever the news makes my heart drop especially, I pull out my pen to try to make you feel near and real – an illogical feeling that I can help you in this nightmare by holding you tightly in my mind. I simply cannot imagine what it can all be like – sometimes for comfort I try to make myself believe that it is better for you in it, with something you can really do [with] no time for thought than it is for me who can do so little for you except cut off your lilac heads and mulch the Doyenne de Comise – it was so heavenly at Broccers yesterday – not really hot but bursts of sunshine and huge towering clouds sailing up on the northern wind. The first glimpse when one arrives makes one gasp – a mass of pale mauve and pale yellow iris leading the eye to the deeper purple of the thyme which is like a solid cushion on the grey, and picks up the more brilliant purpley pink of the peony on the steps, the scale starts of descent to the paler Saponaria and ends in the foam of the cerastium – all that bit really couldn't be more enchanting, luckily there have been a succession of 'guests' all wondering and admiring – I felt quite elated –I stayed over there to supper yesterday and we sat watching the spinney grow gradually darker and then I bicycled slowly home . . . I worked yesterday on the cistus bed . . . it is perfect weeding weather – a gentle sun, a gentle wind and the earth crumbling through one's fingers. I really do think I am as potty about gardening as you are – sometimes it seems almost absurd in this life in real life in earnest times that it should seem so profoundly important *to take out your twitch – but I reason that this garden of ours in something we have made together and it's got a sort of precious quality almost as a child might have.'*

The Spears became increasingly worn down by bedbugs, dysentery, and infection. As the battle for Damascus continued, Humphrey developed an infected hand. Everyone working at the hospital was, in various ways, becoming more debilitated. Humphrey observed that *'Hugh . . . is not well, his belly having given out again. Hammy too is bad, he carries on courageously. No doubt a certain amount as we were warned, was inevitable, but overwork I feel has helped and the shocking sanitary conditions that prevail in our camp. I am pessimistic enough to think if one were less sensitive one would be better adapted to life. This unit is in a manner selected by its sensibility, is that why though all its members are supposed to have passed a stiff medical examination they are breaking down like this? Or is it that an insanitary hospital is more than anyone can stand up against. I was continually running in splinters in Sarafand, none went septic. Hugh went sick there and so did Hammy but only for a day. We knew hardships at Namsos but no one went home.'*

～

Humphrey struggled with his own feelings about what he was doing. Standing as he always had at the periphery of the Establishment, he felt trapped by his situation. The horror of the makeshift Deraa hospital ended when the Vichy French surrendered on the 22nd June. The Spears packed up, left the squalid location and drove north to Damascus. Humphrey's hand was still infected, others in the unit continued to suffer attacks of dysentery

Life in Damascus was a considerable improvement. Their hospital was housed in what had been an Italian convent hospital. It was at least a clean, functioning building. They were able to provide medical help to village communities, treating tuberculosis, malaria and other conditions when they weren't busy with injured soldiers. Compared to Deraa it was a relative pleasure. But the risk of death, even amongst their unit was never far away. In mid-July, on the way to collect medical supplies, two members of the Unit lost control driving round a tight road bend, flipped their vehicle and were flung out of the windows. They were killed instantly. Humphrey set out to retrieve the bodies, dealing with the horror by dissociating into the beauties of nature: 'we *drove down that lovely road through the long, drawn-out Damascus oasis, full of the beauty of olives, till we reached the wide plain under Mount Hermon all gold and violet. We put the bodies in behind on stretchers and drove back . . . we gathered as in a dream some blue salvia-looking flowers – only with a peony fingered leaf – and tucked them into their blankets.*

Time off, away from hospital work, also provided respite, and in Humphrey's case somewhat romantic adventure. '*Hammy and I had a lot of fun: I being romantic, he as practical as possible in perfect real agreement.* In the second week of July, he and Hammy headed to Haifa and Mount Carmel. '*We reached Haifa east and breakfast in an excellent Viennese restaurant. The cold of the hour before dawn had been appalling. Took a taxi the top of Mount Carmel and found a hotel. Our room was charming: very simple: a NW aspect overlooking the sea. The air of Carmel is Champagne or Damascas Retsina would be truer perhaps, piney and delicious, always a breeze, cooled by the sea . . . Our six days passed too quickly. On the last Hammy let me leave the sling off and we bathed in that heavenly warm sea, walking to a quiet part of the beach where our nakedness would pass unnoticed. The custom of the country seemed to be to bathe in drawers and then walk about naked carrying them in the hand. We had no money to buy any so were much pleased to find them unnecessary.*'

~

A few weeks later, on another break, Humphrey joined an expedition to climb Mount Hermon with a cousin of Stephen Verney who was visitingthe Spears. Gardens were never far from his thoughts, and although he regarded the views and colours from the peak through an artist's eye, the detail of the plant species and the flowers he found were just as absorbing. After the climb, John Verney who had been fighting the French outside Damascus 'the previous week or two' was enchanted by Humphrey and wrote to his wife, '*30 July 1941 Humphrey Waterfield is a delightful person . . . I think after brief acquaintance, one of the nicest people I have ever met – very sensitive and also sensible with a pleasant and kind face.*'

~

Further solace came from Nancy, in which her skilful descriptions of his beloved garden flooded Humphrey's mind, momentarily eclipsing the tedium and brutality of war: '*Thursday July 31st The summer nearly gone. Letters from Nancy make one realise how nearly gone it is. It seems to have been an exciting year in the garden. Iris sylosa, the white form, flowered for the first time after about three years. One of the magnolias and the thompsonii also flowered for the first time. The andromdedas seem to have done well: in spite of lime but not the azaleas. The white fritillaries seem to be spreading, on balance an encouraging report, the yellow iris under the laburnum seem to have been lovely and the wisteria, just moved there this winter . . .*'

Humphrey tried to think of the monotony and service to others as a transformative experience and sometimes it even worked, much to his surprise: '*August 16th . . . leaving tomorrow – Yesterday I spent packing the downstairs ward, a pleasant change from ward work. It is difficult to know what one really feels about anything. I always talk about hospital work as if I hated it and indeed I do, as I hate anything which prevents me painting, as I hate routine, as I hate dull menial work. And yet one must admit that on occasions one has now the ecstasy of complete self-abnegation, probably the highest happiness of which the true egoist is capable.*'

~

169

On 15th August 1941, the Spears moved on to Beirut. The first night spent in their new hospital quarters left them riddled and swollen with bed bug bites, several days later, they moved on again, to another hospital in Lebanon, still attending to any wounded troops and dealing with local medical needs. Although they were for the time being no longer in the thick of the battle as they had been in Deraa, unit members continued to fall ill, suffering from what was known as 'three-day fever', recovering enough to work, then becoming ill again. Malaria also affected many of the patients. To cope with it all, Humphrey retreated to musings on Hill Pasture:

'Friday Sept 5th September the world over . . . September is the half deaf, the muffled month, the cock crows down the hill, the sound comes up blurred through veils of damp . . . moreover it has rained, twice perhaps that accounts for my homesickness. I have spent all afternoon walking with Nancy round the garden at Broccers. It will be off season of course the candicans should be looking splendid against high cumulus cloud. There should be an air of growth about everything, very satisfying to the gardener's heart, the fleeting blooms are over the slow more permanent things should now be proving their height: the thuya may have added a foot.'

~

In early 1942, the Spears left the bleak Palestinian landscape *"the dullest stretch yet – yellow unmitigated sand"* and headed west. It was a grim time for the Allies in the war beyond the dry sands of the Middle East. The Axis was flourishing. Hitler dominated Europe; Mussolini was only too pleased to be part of what appeared to be success and was busy throwing his weight around North Africa. Japan had invaded much of south-east Asia, capturing thousands of Allied troops. If military success can be compared to a surgeon surveying the important parts of a human body, 'Desert Fox', Field Marshal Rommel had set his sights on the aorta. He needed to control the port of Tobruk. Once in command of Tobruk, Egypt and, the jewel in crown of control, Suez, could be accessed. And if he could access Suez, he could cut off weapons, fuel and troop transport as far as India. It could be a world-dominating win. Hitler's *Lebensraum* strategy would be amply fulfilled.

~

On 30th January, 1942, the Spears set up a Tobruk field hospital on what seemed to be a random piece of desert sand and began to receive the injured. There was a sense of foreboding. Fighting began and desert patrols brought in wounded men, machine gun fire peppered the air. Humphrey's mood spiralled downwards: '*7th Feb more work more hospitals . . . patients lay in a wallow of filth. Everything went on the floor, every now and again one came on a bottle stinking and encrusted with filth or a bowl of sickness or sputum. Tobruk . . . Feb 8th Monday . . . If it were not for Nancy I wonder if I would not make an end of myself – it would surely be easy to take a syringe of morphia and swim out to sea and would it be wrong? I don't believe in Hitler, I don't believe in Churchill – I dislike one about as much as the other . . . I cannot abide anything I hear on the wireless; everything seems more or less bad . . .*'

~

And all of a sudden, it got much worse. On 14th February, after taking cover in trenches from the shells of a German aeroplane, Spears members emerged to find that Nik Alderson, their leader and Humphrey's oldest friend in the company, who they thought was sheltering safely in his own trench, had been directly hit by a shell. At first the men assumed he had managed to hide somewhere else, but as the dust and sand settled the terrible truth dawned. Nik had been blown apart and the largest remaining piece of him was his arm. The group then began the gruesome task of trying to collect as many bits of Nik as they could, including his liver.

Twenty-three-year old Nik's terrible death hit the men hard.

Humphrey knew without Nik's influence, he might never have joined the FAU. He wrote to Nancy: *'imagine going round collecting bits of that lovely creature – they never found the head at all. Dear Funny, why should these things happen – he was such a part of one's life, so understanding and sympathetic and so affectionate – so devoted to you and I think to us both, at every turn one will miss him.'*

CHAPTER TWENTY-FIVE

Eden's Keeper

1943-1944

'You are my eyes and my heart
and I need them in the right place.'

T he death of Nik Anderson weighed heavily on all members of
the Hadfield Spears; he had seemed so young and so invincible.
A prominent Quaker family member, Mike Rowntree, replaced him
as leader. The battle of Tobruk in May 1942 had been a success for
Rommel and a disaster for the Allies, they would have to wait until
the autumn and the Second Battle of Alamein, before they would
surge successfully through to North Africa under 'Monty' Field
Marshal Montgomery. Examining Humphrey's FAU records, he was
stationed in Tobruk for several months. Although at times he
immersed himself in nostalgic Hagley memoir writing, and wrote
and read letters to and from Nancy, his mood was low; *'Ten days of*
moderate hell . . . temp 99 degrees fortunately went down before evening
instead of up . . . personally I find myself profoundly depressed by the
thought of the future of England. This appalling lack of imagination all

the way . . . the colonel trying to carry on as if in a well-appointed house and peacetime hospital; the Registrar entirely unaware of the situation on the wards; the monstrous exploiting of the men, the eternal reiteration of the meals – boiled potatoes every day for 9 weeks . . . The world needs a new order and if England will not help to give it her someone else will. More than ever do I feel that a British victory would be a disastrous thing. A stalemate is the best we can hope for and world revolution as non-violent as possible.'

⁓

It was now over two years since Nancy and Humphrey had seen each other, and it seemed inconceivable that such a long stretch of time had passed. Her letters from England weren't only about plants and the progress of the trees, they were lyrical letters of tender love. The garden may have been the physical centre of their friendship, but the love they shared, however unusual, was as certain in her mind as the earth in which she planted. *'Truth is I am timid, as you have frequently had occasion to remark, what's worse I do mind very much about my own skin. I used to feel quiet detachment and think I would not at all mind exchanging this world for the next, but now the desire to see you again eclipses any charm the thought of heavenly encounters might have held.'*

⁓

His letters to her were equally loving. He may not have described wanting to feel the warmth of her skin or his lips on hers, but her soul and steady love sustained him, and the garden and Nancy were the future *"I am just homesick for that silly plot of ground and nothing can alter it it. Lots of this country is more beautiful and paintable – one of my plans is to bring you back here and we will hire a car and drive around painting it – And if we can't afford a car, we will have a donkey and you can learn Arabic . . . I would give anything to be back at Broccers and to have seen it this spring."* Nancy's desire to communicate her pleasure in the beauty that surrounded her wasn't always centred on Hill Pasture. The Tennant garden at Orford House was an inspiration too but always in relation to the garden she and Humphrey were creating together: '*The garden here is very beautiful but not as lovely as ours, a tangle of winter taking over from summer. Stock and mignonette smelling delicious, mauve tobacco plant tying up with the Michaelmas daisies. Nutty smells of fallen leaves and the house scarlet with creeper – all the way to Broxbourne I long for you to be with me – the trees so exquisite, half bare so that one can see their form, with sprinkles of gold and russet. I just sat and sat and let my imagination run hopefully away to the time when we should be there together – I wondered what I should cook for lunch – or whether perhaps we shouldn't bother much for you would be working, instead we would have a lovely supper followed by the Schubert Nocturne? Or the Mozart G Major? Meantime, among these impossible dreams there is the reality of your trees growing away as hard as they can.*'

~

Nancy wasn't just pottering about passively, rejoicing in gardening and plant progress. Her role as NFWI Co-chairman required energy, travel and continuous exchange. She lectured around the country at numerous local institutes, broadcasting for the BBC and, at the 1943 NFWI AGM, met the Queen, describing herself as being a *"mass of nerves"* before the event began. '*Darling Funny I have been very grand today. We had a great "thrill" as Her Majesty was graciously pleased to come to the meeting (I've known for some two months but it was a deadly secret). It will seem to you silly womens' stuff but in fact I found it very moving indeed. Lady D [Denham] and three or four of us were in the porch to meet her, I had a long conversation; she had the prettiest face and voice. You see I get grander and grander . . .*'

~

Daily thoughts and longing flowed through the innumerable letters she wrote over the years of Humphrey's Middle Eastern posting.

Letters that for all she knew, might never arrive. Some letters were returned, as there was no certainty of delivery for a mobile hospital address, and weeks of hearing nothing from him made Nancy feel as if she was firing into an abyss. She sent him books, hoping that eventually he might hold them in his hands and find their contents intellectually sustaining. Did they ever arrive? It was impossible to know for months at a time. Sometimes a parcel would turn up in her letterbox. An Egyptian djellaba for instance: '*a superb shimmer of stripes and satin – I sailed about in it feeling ever so sweet . . . dear Funny what was in your mind about it? Are you going to wear it at Broccers when you smoke your hookah or whatever it is? Does a model recline like Omar Khayyam under a willow or does Aunt Nan have it made into an exquisite evening tunic to wear with a velvet skirt?*'

~

Nancy's extended family was growing up. Her niece, Linnet Birley, joined the Navy, her nephew Tom Birley was old enough to join the Army. She wrote to Humphrey of her concerns for Linnet, feeling she was too sensitive a soul for the horrors of war: '*with . . . a sinking heart I saw her off in an Underground train bound for Mill Hill.*' Although Humphrey was at risk of serious illness and death in the Middle East, Nancy's life wasn't without danger either. Staying one night in York for a WI conference, her hotel took a direct hit: '*About 4am sirens went off and simultaneously bombs began to fall. I had difficulty in getting out of my room as the door had jammed through the blast, but when I did emerge it was to confront a heterogeneous collection of curling-pinned, pyjama'd, dressing gowned guests, all trying to find the air raid shelter. There wasn't one so we sat on the stairs leading to the cellar . . . everyone was frightened. The Irish cook had hysterics and buried her head in my lap. The raid only lasted about an hour but we were too cold to go back to bed, so we dressed and joined the crowds pouring into the streets. A full moon lit up the Minster which towered above us, black and enormous against a crimson background of burning houses . . . The conference took place as planned; WI members are not easily deterred.'*

She pined for his physical presence. She longed to give him "a hug". Perhaps a job in Egypt would be a solution of sorts? There was a possibility she could take one. She wrote to him, suggesting it and waited for his reply. It might mean at least she could clap eyes on him. After months, she finally, received his response: *'I shall not attempt to influence your decision because I think it would be very selfish. Lovely though it would be to see you, it would probably be one week and against that one week I should have 51 infinitely poorer. Instead of chat about Broccers, I should have letters as dull as those I write to you because we should both be living intolerable lives and who would mind about the carpenteria or let me see the beauty of the cherries? You are my eyes and my heart and I want to have them in the right place."*

So, the Egypt idea was abandoned, and on she went, travelling around the country for the NFWI, meeting with the great and the good, and when she went home, being loving 'Aunt Nan' to her family and peddling back and forth from Ugley to Hill Pasture on her bicycle: *'I am on my way to Droitwich for 3 days lecturing. It should be rather pleasant in this exquisite weather. Dear Funny, I sometimes feel you will get tired of superlatives but really Broxted on Saturday was a miracle – I bicycled there – the hedges brilliant with privet, dog wood and great scarlet necklaces of berries. Smith has acres of sea green cabbages that link up with the sky, with the bright yellow lichen of this roof, to mark the division. Our little place had completely changed in a week, it fairly took my breath away – the pale gold and grey – what an exquisite mixture, of the poplars and cotoneaster . . .'*

The ebb and flow of Humphrey's relationships in the desert weren't degenerating as swiftly as his optimism for England's future. His estrangement from Hammy came to an end, and he found its rapprochement brought him joy. Like an adolescent girl, he reinstated Hammy into his friendship group: *'It was the first time for long months*

I have had a real talk with Hammy and it was the old Hammy one had loved long since and lost awhile. The 'scrubby schoolboy' aspect fell away and as he warmed to his subject [music] he became transfigured and the angel that is tucked away inside looked out. Today he is the hobbled yokel again, shuffling round the camp about his chores, but last night the competent, sufficient Ham became the beautiful ineffectual angel. I thought irresistibly of the Shelley portraits. It seems only to happen to artists, Nancy, Peter and Hammy. They light one up and 'the veils of the soul therein', nothing perhaps remarkably beautiful in themselves become glowing fragments of the beauty one feels may be the one reality behind the universe.'

~

Humphrey's surroundings didn't always measure up to the flights of romantic fancy in his head. As always, if there was a chance to explore, he took it, either to paint or simply rejoice in the colours and detail of his new surroundings. But one benign stroll heading towards Rosetta turned into a fracas: he was set upon by a mob of local youths, angry that this Westerner wouldn't part with his money: '. . . *stones began to fly, they began to paw me, the degenerate leader to caress my bottom – I quickened my pace, a clod of earth I think it must have been, struck me on the back of the neck; I walked ahead pretending not to have noticed. Both pacifist principle and policy prevented me from offering any violence in which it seemed evident that I could only come off worst . . . But then half bricks began again and one struck me on the calf and brought me to the ground. I struggled limping round a bend I had no idea where I was exactly: Rosetta's minarets shone white, miles in front . . . one hears of soldiers disappearing; an odd body floating in the Nile and who would have been any the wiser? I was deeply grateful to the boatmen round the bend who finally sent the mob packing. I managed to limp the mile or two to the road, got a lift on a lorry back to the camp."* This unpleasant encounter reinforced his argument that Nancy should not, under any circumstances, take up the job offer in Egypt: *'This really is a country of which it really could be said that 'every prospect pleases and only man is vile.'*

~

The tides of war were turning, and change was coming. Rommel's success was countered. Field Marshal 'Monty' Montgomery triumphed by 11th November 1942 in the Second Battle of El Alamein and the first phase of the war ended. The beginning of the end of the war began. As the Allies began to push west from Alamein, they retook Tobruk, surprising everyone by their speed. And then they moved further west. By September 1943, the Spears transferred to give medical backup to the Free French, Deuxième Division Blindée, fighting the North African campaign. The Spears continued west, supporting the push into Tunisia. They moved through the Libyan region of Tripolitania and arrived in Zuwara for a three month deployment. By December 1943, they reached the coastal resort of Hammamet. But in spite of the blue sea and the possibility of pleasant swimming, Humphrey grumbled into his journal, about spending a month on 'nights', *'twenty-eight days from just before Christmas. There was ridiculously little to do – and sometimes it seemed quite ridiculous to torture oneself into remaining awake in order to hand out perhaps two cough lozenges.'* By the time the Spears arrived in Tunis, which in another life, Humphrey might have visited and admired the beauty of nearby Carthage, it was a dismal vision of the aftermath of combat. Tunis was *'a disaster, every 100th soldier drunk on his back. The immense enthusiasm of the inhabitants reduced to apathy and indifference . . . an aerodrome a place of twisted girders and mangled German carrying planes.'*

~

By the spring of 1944, the Allies had taken control of the former Italian and French colonies of North Africa. The Axis Forces were in retreat. Humphrey and his fellow Spears members returned to England in May 1944 where their ship docked in Liverpool with the *Marseillaise* playing loudly to greet the Free French with their national anthem. By the time he arrived home to Hill Pasture, not only was Nancy by his side, but the nightingales had struck up. Just as they had on his return from Scandinavia in 1940, now their haunting warbles drifted across the darkness once more. After years of heat, dust, sand and the blood of friends and strangers, he could luxuriate in what Nancy had achieved in his absence. Hill Pasture had matured in the three years since Humphrey had last seen it. The place he had left had not remained a memory but was a living, beautifully planted Eden, loved and nurtured by his friend, just as she loved him. He was granted two days leave before being sent to Hull for three months, reunited with the Friends Ambulance Unit. Nancy would have to continue to "love and cherish" Hill Pasture on her own for a good while yet.

CHAPTER TWENTY-SIX

Prisoner of War

1944

*'I shall cherish and love your garden – the bit by the
pond a miracle of autumn enchantment, scarlet and gold,
the valley blue with haze and willows silver, the hedges
are hung with old man's beard . . . some day we
shall come together again . . .'*

While most of Europe began to rejoice at the success of the
1944 Normandy Landings, with the end of the war in sight,
Humphrey was incarcerated; a starving prisoner of war in Eastern
France.

After three months in Hull, and following the success of the
D Day Landings, still attached to the Deuxième Division Blindée,
Humphrey's Unit had followed the Allied convoy to France, arriving
in liberated Paris. Swept along by thousands, the Unit cheered and
kissed its way through the ecstatic crowds. Free and happy as the
Parisians were, further east, towards the German border, the war was
still being fought in a series of retreats and minor victories. Humphrey

and his driver, Ray Bartlett, provided medical back up as they moved towards the Grand Est region. Ordinarily they, like the Red Cross, would be exempt from capture, as they were saving the lives of any casualties, whichever side they were fighting on. The ambulances acted as make-shift operating theatres, threading their way behind the lines down side roads and unmarked tracks. One September evening, after shelling and gunfire began, the Unit picked up an injured group: '*There were five in this little lot, four Germans one Frenchman. We bandaged them as best we could in the back of the ambulance . . . suddenly there was a clamour of raucous Germans' voices and we were forced out, one on each side.*'

Humphrey and Ray were rounded up with the men they had been treating. Humphrey tried his best, dredging up German that he hadn't used for two decades, imploring the German commander to allow them to drive the seriously injured to a hospital. But it was not to be. They were all "bundled" into the back of the ambulance together. Even then, the child in Humphrey found something to be delighted by: '*There was a charming moment: French, English and German, we all melted into one common humanity. The Frenchman who was on a stretcher because we were a French ambulance, gave up his stretcher to the more seriously wounded German, the German needing our pressure to take it.*'

∽

They were taken from one make-shift prison to another. Arriving at the border town of Colmar, a taste of what was to come hit them: '*we . . . found ourselves for the first time up against the real thing: a howling mob of prisoners greeted us from the endless rows of windows of a lofty disused factory, Poles, Italians, Russians all yelling a welcome to the new faces . . .*'. He and Ray eventually ended up in Strasbourg. '*An unpleasant Obergefreiter with an obscene looking stump of a left arm searched us and we were brought to a cage already full of French and Americans in two vaults under the mound of an 1870 fortification.*'

The crowding was so bad in Strasbourg there was barely enough space to lie down. They remained in the vaults for two days until the number of prisoners became so great, they were moved to an old French military hospital. Here they were given their own rooms, and even had the luxury of running water. The more serious problem began with the rations they were given to eat. Coffee for breakfast, a watery vegetable soup for lunch and bread and jam for supper, day after day after long day. Soon the prisoners began to starve: '*The guards tried their best to mitigate the system they had to enforce, it became regular practice for Ray to collect what remained of the German soup in the evening from the corporal's mess and from time to time they would bring us bits of bread.*'

Humphrey's talent for dissociation, his apolitical standpoint and lack of religion helped him survive, and made him better able to empathise with the common humanity shared with his fellow prisoners and the guards. As the weeks dragged on, he was put to work as a hospital orderly. Because they were living and working in a hospital, they were not official prisoners of war, even though they were incarcerated. In some ways, it was even worse than being a POW. Letters and critically, food parcels could not reach them. They were so hungry they tried not to mention food, but their dreams were suffused with it. Nancy tried to write to him but her letters were returned. '*I shall cherish and love your garden – the bit by the pond a miracle of autumn enchantment, scarlet and gold, the valley blue with haze and willows silver, the hedges are hung with old man's beard . . . some day we shall come together again . . .*' she wrote, not knowing if he would ever read it.

~

He had to make do with his imagination: '*And so we missed yet another autumn: the little maple tree one could just see from one lavatory daring to do duty for all the autumn colour of the world. And there were snow-berries in a corner of the courtyard and the sky. As a pacifist I was glad of the experience, glad to experience hunger, glad to pass through the looking glass, to find a world, oh so like our own, propaganda so exactly mirroring propaganda; only as is the way with mirrors, the image a tone or two lower than our own . . .'* On the 23rd November 1944, Le Clerc's Armoured Division captured Strasbourg and flew the French flag from the Cathedral. The Germans were in retreat. The hospital Camp Commandant asked Humphrey to lead the surrender from the building. Waving a sheet attached to a broomstick, he, Ray and the Commandant walked into central Strasbourg and into freedom.

Nancy was standing on the platform of Baker Street Underground station when the news of Humphrey's release reached her: *'my eye fell on Stop Press news in the Evening Standard, 'H Waterfield had been found in Strasbourg'. It seemed impossible not to proclaim the news to everyone in sight'.* By the time she had returned to Ugley that evening, her mother and sister were waiting for her on the front door steps. What a long way her beloved mother had come in recognition and respect of her daughter's loving friendship. The Friends Ambulance Unit had sent a message about his release to Orford. It was joyful news indeed.

Humphrey didn't come home straight away; he and Ray were admitted to hospital as soon as they returned to England. After months of semi-starvation, their bodies were emaciated and weak. Medical supervision was required for the initial days of normal food intake. And then, ten days after his arrival, he rang the London offices of the WI. Nancy didn't answer the phone herself, a man's voice asked to speak to Miss Tennant. As she lifted the receiver to her ear, a loved, familiar voice told her he was at Victoria Station. Could she come? She rushed to meet him.

The very first thing Humphrey wanted to do when he returned to Essex with Nancy was visit Hill Pasture. Standing, staring at it in the December light, he knew it had become proper garden. Not bursting with the energy and flamboyance of a Hill Pasture in spring or summer, but a heavenly vision of the sleepy, simple peace of an

English garden in the deep mid-winter. At that time of year, it was quiet and still. Humphrey's living composition of vistas and views beyond greeted him like old friends. Bare branches stretching across the sky, the weak December sun making soft shadows on the grass, the dark green of the yew and brighter green of thuya giving contrived elegance and order. He envisaged spending the day working on the garden again and was happy. Hand, head and heart reunited in the place that gave him greatest happiness. However, he was still weak and by the end of the day he had to retire early to bed. He was given a month to recuperate, which was not enough time in Nancy's opinion.

Even if the war seemed over, its aftermath required enormous operational manpower from the Allies. Humphrey was called up again, this time with the French Division and sent to Bavaria to supervise the establishment of peace after the end of the war. This was not pleasant. After Germany's defeat, the wide-scale rape of German women, initially believed to be by the Soviet Army, but latterly by Allied troops too, was widespread. Nancy puts the horror delicately: *'his job was to try and save the German ladies from the depredations of the French soldiery. This was a delicate and difficult task in which he finally had to get the co-operation of his Commanding Officer. The gratitude of the German ladies knew no bounds.'*

Both he and Raymond were awarded the Croix de Guerre, the French medal of honour for those who supported the French Allies. Humphrey refused the medal but accepted the citation, displaying instead his pacifist credentials in flying colours. Finally in 1945, he was demobilised early, on the condition he signed on for agricultural work. And so he did – in a way. A large bed of potatoes in the gulley at Hill Pasture required Humphrey's urgent attention. Again, just as they had before the war, he and Nancy were able to plant and plan. At the same time, his thoughts began to drift to France, to Le Clos and to Pau. He and his brother Tony ought to go and see what remained.

CHAPTER TWENTY-SEVEN

Paradise Reimagined

1946

The gulley's potato crop had been harvested. That part of the garden would now become an iris bed. Nancy and Humphrey were daring to think not simply the weeks ahead, but months and years. But now it was time to return to France. Humphrey set off with his brother Tony and sister-in-law, Honor. First stop was Pau where they would visit Barbara and Derick's final home, La Jouvence. They would also visit their graves in Pau.

~

When they arrived, it was comforting to find that Barbara and Derek's servants, Emma and Victorine, the loyal unfortunates who dealt with the aftermath of the double suicide, were still living in the house. It had been a long six years since Humphrey had seen them, but it was consoling in part, to discover that they had weathered the war and were in reasonable spirits. Not all had been lost or forgotten. Barbara and Derek's wish that their servants would be provided for and survive had at least been fulfilled. But the main mission was Menton. Would Le Clos even still exist in any version of its previous incarnation? They knew the town had been shelled from the sea. And even if it were still standing, would anything within it remain? They knew it had been commandeered by Italian officers and after they left, refugees had sheltered in the building.

〜

As the brothers walked up the drive to the front of Le Clos, it was like stepping back in time: the sensation of dry olive leaves crunching beneath their feet; the sound of the sea washing over the shingle in the bay; the scent of the clement, marine air mixed with sun scorched herbs. The villa towered above them, looking defiantly solid. At first glance, the outside of the late nineteenth century building looked reasonably intact. The honey-coloured exterior still stood, undamaged. Its balconies on the first and second floors looked as grand and as elegant as they had always done. Wrought ironwork window boxes graced smaller windows. A few panes of glass appeared to be missing or cracked here and there, and there were small signs of mortar damage, but no obvious, cataclysmic scars of war. Rambling roses still tumbled over the portico: the wisteria looked even more rumbustious. Most of the garden had disappeared, lost under a tangle of weeds and overgrown shrubs: what was once a place of horticultural order had become a Mediterranean wilderness. The fundamentals were still there: the grotto, the six terraces leading down from the top of sloped land behind the villa, the pond his mother had created, though choked with plants, was still a pond. The two palm trees, *Washingtonia filifera* and *Nolina*, that the brothers had loved from childhood, had grown to be enormous.

〜

But it was like visiting a memory of a house in a day-dream. The people who should have been there were absent. No Betty Duff to greet them warmly; no requirement to gargle or wash hands before entry to appease Barbara. For the first time, they could walk straight into the building without having to comply with their mother's 'malade imaginaire' restrictions and without being worried they were late for the next formal dining arrangement. But where the exterior's appearance was a relief, the interior was far more depressing. Evidence of the war years and neglect was everywhere. The past elegance, order and scrupulous cleanliness had been replaced with a sordid chaos.

~

Abandoned buildings smell. Some have a benign, slightly smothering scent of old plaster, dust and damp. Others can be far worse. Le Clos smelt terrible. It was infested with rats. The Waterfield brothers found themselves staring at room after room of broken furniture, walls scrawled with *grafitti* and vermin-gnawed piles of abandoned books. The waxy glue used to bind them had proved to be a banquet for the mice. The exuberant carelessness of the requisitioned Italian officers was evident; throwing their youthful weight around, tripping over clumsily after too much to drink, flicking their cigarette ends into the once grand fireplaces. And then pitiful to imagine the ensuing refugees, making the best of living in a carcass of a house with what little possessions they might have cobbled together, enduring bombardment while the war raged.

~

It was time to go outside again. They began to wander further into what had been the garden, all so familiar, but altered by years of neglect. But then, in places, amongst the sprawling plants and over-grown shrubs, they began to notice order. Weeding appeared to have been done. Someone was trying to look after the garden. Mario Lavagna had returned. The young gardener who had known the brothers since childhood, who had begun working with his father at Le Clos at the age of fourteen, was now a wizened, wiry looking man of almost fifty. He and his wife had been evacuated to Marseilles during the war, but now they were back, and he was trying his best to tame the tangled jungle of a garden.

⁓

Travelling back to a childhood home after years of absence plays tricks with the mind. The familiarity is so intense, it seems impossible to believe so many years or even months have elapsed since the last sighting. Looking at what remained of the garden, towards the villa with its grand balustrades, the wisteria and the palm leaves swaying in the slight breeze as they always had against the blue Mediterranean sky, neither the Waterfields nor Mario could view Le Clos objectively. How could Humphrey separate himself from his memories of childhood: he and his little brother, playing in their sailor suits; the young Oxford undergraduate arriving back for the holidays or the Bloomsbury artist, arriving in Menton with Nancy for the first time? He couldn't.

⁓

Should they sell it? Tony would find the money useful, with a young wife and family to look after. An agent in the town had offered £1000. But Humphrey felt differently. He couldn't let it go. So much of what he felt and who he believed himself to be was rooted in the place. His day-dream of the irises at Le Clos while he lay in the Scandinavian sun briefly transporting him away to something beautiful; the memory of the scent of Mediterranean flowers wafting through his nursery window as a small boy. Le Clos and the garden were part of who he had once been and still felt himself to be. *The Trees* wasn't just about Hagley and an English garden paradise, it was about France too. The gardens of his childhood had formed him: *'He went with Mademoiselle to her campagne, the great bassin below the cypress trees, was introduced to Joseph feeding the goats in the dark vault beneath the vine leaf arbour who gave him slips of lilac, a white one and a mauve, that he planted in the stony soil of his own plot. And if these failed in comfort, there was the mounded cherry tree, whose silken furbelows brushed the Mediterranean blue with a touch caressing as Renoir's, pink and tremulous beneath the olive trees, as clear and precise and sensuous as painting on the most delicate of porcelain.'*

He decided to save the garden and remodel the house into flats. These would be rented out, or sold on a long lease, and the income would support the overall running costs. Re-designing the garden would be his next project. He would breathe new life into Le Clos and apply his creative imagination. The best of the past would remain, and the sadness could be overcome by new planting, configurations and vistas. He would bring energy into the house, and eventually, the melancholic ghosts of the past would disappear. He would plant bulbs and lilies as his mother had. He would use the views of the sea and the mountains behind. He would pay homage to the exotic as well as the beautiful. Humphrey began to plan what would become one of the most famous gardens on the French Riviera. Mario had returned to restore the garden and so would he. And it would be another place for him and Nancy to delight in.

~

He decided to divide the garden into zones. The higher terraces became the 'Mediterranean Zone'. Here he planted iris, spirea, cherry and Judas trees. On the lower terraces, he created the 'Mexico Zone' with Agave, Bechuriana, Mesembryantheum. He created a 'scala nobile' or water staircase', not on the scale of the colossal creation he and Nancy had admired near Naples on their happy holiday together in the 1930's, but a central water feature, of five descending pools, inviting the observer from the top terrace down through the garden and drawing the eye up to a sixth pool, the sea, beyond. Another magnolia grandiflora would go in. A swimming pool was built, framed by two cypress trees, drawing the eye up to the mountains that rose behind Menton. He would connect the

Mediterranean with the Mexican zone by planting arches of Italian Pencil Cypress.

~

It was all made harder because finances were limited, not simply because Humphrey had little money to lavish but also because currency restrictions prevented much money being taken out of Britain. He was fortunate in his cousin and neighbour, Lylu Hennessy. She had returned to Menton after the war and was on hand to help with overseeing the project when he wasn't in France. Another Menton neighbour, Maybud Campbell a former opera singer, enthusiastic botanist and plantswoman, helped him too. The land surrounding her palatial villa, Val Rameh, burst with exotic flora, and her particular love was nightshades. She gave Humphrey plants and guidance.

~

The elegant marble staircase remained at the back of the house allowing the tenants to access their different areas. New entrance doors to the individual flats at the back of the building were added. But the front elevation stayed the same, so that the glorious balcony upon which that Nancy had felt "demoralised by pleasure" in the 1930's would continue to look as it always had. They could continue to languish in the sun on it for as long as they pleased. Dividing the villa into flats was not only economically sensible, it also expanded their circle of friends who could then rent the apartments on long lets: *'TS Eliot, the Stracheys, Sir Robert and Lady Meyer, Clive Bell and Barbara Bagenal, thanks to whom we had a memorable tea party with Vanessa Bell and Duncan Grant.'* recalled Nancy. Clive Bell was a friend who was, as a distinguished art critic, supportive of Humphrey's painting but also better known to posterity as a leading figure in the Bloombury group and Vanessa Bell's husband. Nancy was quite struck by Vanessa's beauty. *'I have never forgotten the beauty of her 80-year-old face under a battered black straw hat'.* Duncan Grant, Vanessa Bell's partner, father of her daughter Angelica, and openly gay Bloomsbury artist, delighted Humphrey by professing to be wholly uninterested in seeing the garden, but keen to see his paintings.

∼

A new era for Le Clos unfolded and would become part of Nancy and Humphrey's annual migration for decades to come. As the years rolled by, Humphrey's reputation as an artist, gardener and plantsman increased. He was asked to work on other Mediterranean gardens, including Val Rahmeh and Villa Colfranco, in Lucca. And he had further plans for his English paradise too. It was to be expanded on the most exciting scale.

CHAPTER TWENTY-EIGHT

Fruits of Labour

1946-1950

'I sometimes wondered whether all the singing was really rather absurd, but I came to realise it was important.'

Horizons were beginning to broaden, and Nancy and Humphrey were happy to stretch them further. Nancy could have disappeared into a rarefied, retrograde world, peopled by those from the same background, but she didn't. After the war ended, her work for the NFWI continued and expanded. In her capacity as Chairman of the International Committee, she travelled to Europe again. She was invited to Paris to lecture and broadcast in French, representing the NFWI, discussing what all women could contribute to and benefit from in the organisation. Just as the Government had utilized the NFWI network for evacuating children and producing the nation's jam, they now looked to the International Committee to try to improve Anglo German relations after the war. This was more easily said than done. When hosting a group of German women in England, the guests asked Nancy to communicate their experience of suffering during the war to the British WI members: *'This made me realise a good deal of briefing was necessary before they were let loose on their already none-too-keen to be welcoming hostesses in the Counties.'*

Nancy's ambition to showcase women's voices evolved from being a cheerful musical communion for women as part of every Womens' Institute meeting, to something far larger and more profound. In 1946, the first AGM of the NFWI after the war, assembled in The Royal Albert Hall and Nancy was asked to conduct, opening with the singing of *'Jerusalem'.* The Queen, as Patron of the WI, sat directly behind her: *'I cannot begin to describe how small and ineffective I felt with the organ behind me and five thousand singers in front.'* recalled Nancy.

~

By 1948, Nancy had aired an "idea that had been simmering in my mind for years": to gather together the largest number of WI choirs to sing, and to sing to an exemplary standard. In February 1948, in her capacity as Chairman of the Music and Dancing Sub-Committee, she requested the National Federation of Womens' Institutes hold a Music Festival. The NFWI moved swiftly in backing the proposal. A series of local Festivals in March and April 1950 would be held, followed by county Festivals and finally, the London Festival would comprise of three choirs from each county. When Nancy conceived the idea, she optimistically estimated perhaps ten thousand members might sign up for auditions, in the event, twenty-two thousand members auditioned. Nothing like this had ever been attempted before. *'I sometimes wondered whether all the singing was really rather absurd, but I came to realise it was important'* she recalled.

~

Of course, it was important. Even now, over seventy-five years later, the determination to give women a platform to be truly heard, even if symbolically, is a drum that continues to beat and remains the most fundamental of feminist principals. Whether performing as a body of sound in the 1950 Music Festival, or campaigning for equal pay for men and woment as the NFWI did in the 1940's, despite their floral print dresses and sensible shoes, the members of the NFWI were steely in their determination for progress. They would be heard.

~

The Festival took two years to organise. A new sub-committee was formed purely for music, the Singing Festival Ad Hoc Sub-Committee, with Nancy and three other women in charge. The composer and conductor, Ralph Vaughan Williams, at seventy-eight years old, was persuaded to write the music. His progressive background and belief that music should be accessible to anyone regardless of their education, coupled with prodigious talent and interest in folk songs, made him the obvious choice. The result was *"Songs for All Seasons"*. Hundreds of choirs auditioned for selection, and eventually fifty-nine were picked. They were chosen on merit not geography, some counties contributed a number of choirs to the final Festival, others none. Women travelled from all over the country, some through the night, to get to London.

On the 15th June, 1950, the spectacle and sound of ordinary women, lined up in their hundreds in The Royal Albert Hall, singing their hearts out, and singing very well, in their capacity as village choirs, wasn't simply about music. It shone a light on the vast organisation that had helped hold the fabric of British society together during the war. They were not rarefied creatures of stage and screen. Short, tall, fat or thin, beautiful or not, middle-aged, elderly or young, they would be the same women who had taken the children of strangers into their rural homes, fed them, washed their clothes and preserved the nation's fruit. Sir Adrian Boult conducted the programme until the final chorus, when Vaughan Williams rose to his feet and raised his baton. It was a celebration of the ordinary rising to the challenge of doing something extraordinary. The Times music critic, reportedly, sat in his seat with tears pouring down his face. Nancy described it *'as the only thing in my long life that I can think of as something of an achievement.'*

~

Humphrey and Nancy had another project bubbling. In 1956, she decided to buy Ashgrove Cottage, in Broxted, the land of which backed onto the top of Hill Pasture. She could rent the house out and Humphrey could use the land in the attached paddock to complete 'his vision' for their English paradise. She gave the land to Humphrey. *'The paddock ran across the top of our garden and Humphrey immediately began to transform it. For a time, it was stark and we wondered what he was getting at but after a few years everything fell into place, and because it was sunnier, and could grow more tender plants, it became his favourite part of the garden'* explained Nancy.

~

Humphrey had made some money: not an experience he was ordinarily familiar with. His private income, which had never been enough to do more than keep his dilapidated car on the road and cover his costs of living at Hill Pasture and Menton, had dwindled to a trickle. But thanks to a suggestion from a neighbour, he had been lucky with an investment in television shares. He could now afford to build another storey, a studio floor onto his house. He added luxurious additions to the existing garden as well.

~

In the original part of Hill Pasture's garden he installed a 'Temple of Love', a metal-domed faux Greek temple, offering a spot for contemplation, with a small pond below it. The tension between the contrived order of the garden and the natural beauty of the valley falling away beyond was a master stroke. Once seated in the Temple of Love, the visitor's eye could wander lazily to a new 'Bathing Pool Garden': a swimming pool surrounded by sections of reclaimed wrought iron trellis, eventually covered in climbing roses and clematis. He added an ornate, octagonal lead tank, with a fountain, which he positioned beneath a weeping willow tree. The grey of the lead and the soft, silvery green of the fluttering underside of willow blended into one harmonious, muted palette.

~

Just as he had persuaded Nancy to stand holding a feather duster pretending to be a tree in the 1930's, by the late 50's, Nancy was his partner in the planning of what he called his Moon Gate. He made a large cardboard version of the planned brick construction, and with Nancy's help, manoeuvred it about in the new part of the garden to ensure that the view from both sides - one of the garden within, and one of the valley beyond - was perfectly framed. By the early 1960's, the famous plantsman and writer Lanning Roper had visited Hill Pasture and eulogised about Humphrey's talent in Country Life: *'It has literally been carved from Essex farm and woodland . . . it has been conceived by an artist, who has thought in terms of a series of pictorial landscape compositions . . . there is a curious blending of Riviera and English gardening, revealing an understanding and affection for the elements of both . . .'*

~

Roper's description reads like a mix of poetry and a horticultural index: *'There is a grey and silver garden, with a curving path winding through borders of flowering shrubs such as Senecio greyi, Hibiscus syriacus, ceanothus, buddleias, Xanthorceras sorbifolia and acanthus, with fastigate ever-greens making strong vertical accents and a central wide-spreading paulownia with huge heart-shaped leaves. Woolly-leaved verbascums, the silver filigree of artemisias, giant steely grey thistles, blue Salvia uligimosa, furry felted Stachys lanata and mounds of pinks contrast with the spiky blue-green swords of irises and the series of Madonna and regale lilies that have bold flower form.'*

~

Interest in the garden grew over the years. Humphrey and Nancy held garden open days at Hill Pasture, sometimes with up to three hundred visitors at a time. As Margaret's children became young adults, Nancy's extended family began to expand. She found herself holding the next generation of babies and children: new affections for her great nephews and nieces were forged. As these children grew up, a visit to Hill Pasture, to find Humphrey painting, wearing a large straw hat, was part of their life. Margaret Birley, grand-daughter of Margaret, remembers the joy of his swimming pool: *'The main focal point of Hill Pasture for us as children was the pool, where I and my three siblings learned to swim. We always ran through the garden to reach it, gathering speed during the final yards downhill on a path flanked by rather fragrant snowberry bushes. I'll never forget my brother's intense concentration as he taught himself to swim, propelling himself forcefully from one side of the pool to another. I mostly lazed around in the water, sitting on the steps in the shallow end.'*

When visitors to the Hill Pasture garden followed the route that Humphrey had so carefully planned, they were surprised and delighted by the deliberate vistas and hidden gardens that opened up to them. Humphrey's skill was to engage children with the journey through the garden too. *'Another attraction was the two rose-covered raised platforms at the moongate end of the garden that looked out over fields. My sister and I would each stand on one of them gazing out at the view,'* recalled Margaret Birley.

Ernest Tennant, his war years and first marriage behind him, had remarried and settled back into life quietly at Orford House as the head of the family, enjoying the company of his children, grand-children and extensive butterfly collection. However, there were still ripples in the aftermath of war for him to address as well. At the Nuremberg Trials, Ribbentrop had asked for Ernest to be called to defend him. In '*True Account*', published in 1957, Ernest wrote: '*I am glad that I was disallowed as a witness and in no way involved in his trial, because now when I think of Ribbentrop, I cannot help remembering about the man I knew well and worked with in 1933, 1934 and 1935, rather than the completely altered person he later became and whom I hardly knew at all.*'

$\sim$

Ernest's association with the man Ribbentrop became was dismissed as irrelevant. The Deputy Chief Prosecutor for Britain, Sir David Maxwell Fyfe, declared: '*with regard to this witness . . . the matters for which he is sought to be called are surely the acme of irrelevance. It is submitted that the witness can testify that in the early and middle thirties the defendant asked him to bring him into contact with Lord Baldwin, Mr MacDonald and Lord Davidson, for the purpose of negotiating with the latter toward paving the way to good political relations, aiming at the conclusion of an alliance . . .*'

$\sim$

Just as the generations were shifting in rural Essex, they were also evolving in the London Tennant boardroom. Nancy's parents had died within five years of each other: William Tennant mid-war in 1941; Agnes, in 1946. The 19th century, essentially Scottish Tennant and Gairdner generation was slipping into the past, forming the bedrock of family history and temperament rather than memory for the new youngest members. Ernest had been Chairman of C Tennant, Sons & Co Ltd since 1932, succeeding his father who had been Chairman in 1920. In the 1950's the position was held by the head of the Tennant dynasty, the 2nd Baron Glenconner, Christopher. Ernest's only son Julian had also joined the family firm, along with Christopher's son, the flamboyant, party-loving, Colin Tennant. He would eventually succeed his father, Lord Glenconner, to the title and would become best known for his development of Mustique as an exclusive holiday island, his friendship with Princess Margaret and his genius for throwing glamorous parties.

~

By the end of the 1960's, Nancy, now in her seventies, Humphrey, in his late fifties, still planted and planned, in England and in France, rejoicing in the beauty of the gardens that surrounded them. Humphrey's talent for garden design was also in demand. As his reputation grew, he was commissioned to create a garden at Grey's Court in Oxfordshire and at Abbots Ripton in Yorkshire. He wasn't interested in the fee but took on commissions when they interested him. He also made sure Nancy's own garden at her house, The Chase, followed the same principles of structure as at Hill Pasture: a palette of gentle whites, silvers and greens; an invitation to look beyond the immediate garden space to the world beyond.

'It was positioned to use the 'borrowed landscape' of the surrounding countryside by means of a ha-ha between the main lawn and a large grassy field beyond. Towards the narrow end of the tapering lawn, which formed about a quarter of the garden was a small laburnum tree with an urn nearby, a focal point. At the end of the lawn were two parallel beds of iris and beyond them a beech hedge delineating the boundary between the garden and the field. One of his innovations was the building of a summer house at the wide end of the lawn, which looked west out over it and over the fields beyond the garden. Between the summerhouse and the house itself was a whitewashed wall supporting a wonderful Carpenteria californica and a 'Pink Perfection' rose that lived up to its name. Beyond the kitchen door of the house and to the right of the main lawn was a bed full of snowdrops in the spring, later overshadowed by tall shrubs including white lilac and philadelphus. A narrow flight of steps led down to a small rectangular lawn enclosed by a cypress hedge, with iris in the bed opposite and a small lead tank.

To the right of this was wide grass path between beds of sinuous outline, providing a vista onto another urn at the end of the garden. The beds were full of flowers and shrubs including roses and hemarocallis, ceonothus.'   Margaret Birley

As the years rolled by, their appetite for revelling in beauty, whether in their own gardens or while travelling together was undiminished. Nancy referred their happy state as "a marriage of true minds". In 1971, after yet another familiarly joyful autumn jaunt to Europe, they would return in time for another garden opening at Hill Pasture. And this time, Paul Miles, landscape designer and National Trust garden advisor, was coming. He had heard that Hill Pasture was "the most beautiful small garden in England" and wanted to see it for himself.

CHAPTER TWENTY-NINE

The Wrong Side of the Road

1971

'I felt Humphrey was looking at his lost youth.'

They couldn't avoid thinking about it any longer. For all its beauty, fame and accolade, one day, possibly even quite soon, Hill Pasture would become too much. Humphrey found day to day maintenance dull compared with the creative satisfaction of planning and planting. He couldn't afford expensive gardeners and it would eventually become too physically demanding. Nancy was already in her seventies. Even though Hill Pasture was planted to minimise high intensity gardening with Humphrey's clever choice of shrubs rather than endless flower beds, it was still several acres that required horticultural dedication and hard physical effort. They began to discuss the possibility that eventually, their "earthly paradise" would need to be sold.

~

By 1971, they had been together for nearly four decades. Nancy still felt their 'miraculous friendship' was as fresh and joyful as it had been when she first met the 24 year old artist and fell in love. Their October European holiday had followed the familiar, much-loved pattern: time at Le Clos and touring beautiful places. In 1971, Florence was on the itinerary. Even at the age of seventy-four, she felt just as excited by his company as a love-struck teenager. Their life together was still, after decades, magically happy. '*How to capture rapture? How to pin down in words the blue and gold of sky and buildings, the reflection of light and colour and our enjoyment of each other?*'

~

They had settled into their own version of loving, companionable, intellectually and aesthetically stimulating bliss. After the romantic colour and pomp of Florence they made their way north through France to Bourgogne-Franche-Comté. Humphrey wanted to show Nancy the town of Vézelay. They climbed the austere, steep streets of The Crusader's holy town, up and up to the Romanesque Abbey. Of course, as he always did, Humphrey enhanced the whole experience. He was still, even as a middle-aged man with a softening double chin, her 'perfect Ciccerone'.

~

They arrived back in England after an overnight ferry crossing from Le Havre and left the Southampton docks in the soft autumn light of an October morning. They were Essex bound, travelling past Winchester and through the South Downs that Humphrey as a young man had loved with such intensity. The steep landscape soon gave way to flatter Berkshire fields and dense woodland. They were heading towards Windsor. It was impossible for Humphrey not to glance at the castle without thinking about his schooling, with his old school chapel dominating the view across the flat Thames valley landscape surrounding it. He couldn't resist a spontaneous moment of nostalgia. He had slightly overshot but it wasn't too late. Why not try to pack as much as possible into what is always a rather dull journey home after a holiday? Slamming his car into reverse, he backed up the main road and headed towards Eton College.

~

The ancient buildings of his alma mater came into view as they drove towards the centre of the town. Down the main road, they sped, past the lane that he and his friend Cas had sauntered down as teenagers, Cas laughing at him. On past the playing fields, past the medieval red brick walls and then into the centre of the school. Decades had passed since his time there, but the familiarity of the place was still acute. Memories flooded back: going to the wrong house when he had first arrived, racing through the streets of the town in the 1920's, late for something, probably missing something or losing something, but generally excited.

~

Humphrey Waterfield had lived a full life. His youth was long gone and he was resolutely middle-aged. But as he stood and watched the sons of the next generation, the noise they made was so familiar. Hearing their mixed voices, some high, others broken and mature, chattering and calling out to each other was like travelling back in time. They still behaved towards each other in the same way as his contemporaries had. Some were ragging about as they walked down the pavement in a group; others in calm, companionable silence, some walking alone. It was male youth, in all its variety, running, shouting and moving past them. Perhaps Humphrey and Nancy might have been mistaken for grandparents that day: a woman in her mid-seventies, a man in his early sixties, islands in the middle of an unending stream of boys. Still in the same black tailcoats that Humphrey had worn, but with more self-assurance. These boys with their longer 1970's hair, had a freer, more nonchalant air. The stiffness and formality of the past had gone. Nancy wasn't sure why

204

Humphrey wanted to watch them but she felt '*he was watching his lost youth.*'

~

Was it really a lost youth? Had he not done everything he had set his mind to? He would have liked to have been a recognised artist. Clive Bell had given him an exhibition in London, and had written generous words about his talent, but it hadn't been the great career that his contemporaries at The Ruskin or The Slade had enjoyed. But there was no doubt he was increasingly recognised as a creative genius in garden design and was a known 'artist gardener'. A few years later, in 1976, Hugh Johnson would describe him as '*the most sensitive and original designer of gardens of the last generation.*' The truth was, he had been like the Sassoon bird of his youth, 'winging wildly across the white orchards and dark green fields', going where and doing what he wanted his entire life. He achieved his First, he had become an artist, he remained true to his principles in war. He hadn't fathered children, but he loved his nephews and niece, and he loved Nancy's family too. Perhaps he had remained too much in his 'ivory tower', admiring and loving from afar, never quite declaring his hand, or was it something else? Homosexuality had only recently been legalised. If he had been born at another time, with a slightly different, less sensitive disposition, might he have lived a very different life? Was Hill Pasture a consolation for everything he had lost or couldn't openly have? Was his yearning for Hagley so profoundly ingrained in his psyche that he had spent his entire life chasing the ghost of a childhood garden in his head, refusing to grow up emotionally for fear of abandoning the innocent joys of childhood wonder? He didn't tell Nancy what he was thinking.

~

The 31st October was bright and sunny: perfect autumn weather to enjoy another garden opening of Hill Pasture. The landscape was especially easy to appreciate on a crisp autumn day. No distraction of flamboyant, blousy, aromatic flowers, no scent to seduce the observer into an olfactory reverie of philadelphus, tree peony and rose. The bare bones of the planting were exposed and in turn displayed the genius of the design. Golden, orange, russet and brown, autumn leaves were still hanging in some of the trees, berries punched scarlet and claret red into what remained of the garden before it descended into the monotone of winter. There was a new addition to Hill Pasture to admire: a bronze statue of a shepherd boy, holding a single flower, placed at the top of the garden. Slightly camp was this statue, but the romantic sentiment was powerful. A child, delighting in a flower, holding it aloft as an invitation to enjoy, its Puckish face looking playfully out. It was exactly what Humphrey had achieved on a grand scale. It was also who he felt he was.

~

The most beautiful small garden in England was indeed beautiful that Sunday. Visitors milled about, winding their way through the garden, following Humphrey's route. It was impossible to look at Hill Pasture without thinking about how much Nancy was a part of it. She had been the trees before they were planted; she had loved and cherished the garden in his years of absence; she had provided more land to complete his vision with the moongate and reflective pool. She had been, and still was, his eyes and heart, and he was her beloved. The garden was like their child, but instead of being their combined flesh and blood, it was a living composition of trees, shrubs and flowers.

~

Humphrey rose early the next day. He had to drive to Norfolk to look at a new garden project. Perhaps tired by the garden opening, he was in a muddle. He couldn't find his keys. He was used by now to losing things, he had done it all his life, but at least he knew he could hot wire his car. A screwdriver could do it. He succeeded. It would be fine, but better to collect his spare set from a local garage in Great Easton. He was running later than he should have been and now he was rushing. His mind might have been in France. Was he thinking of Le Clos? Or was it somewhere else entirely? The gardens, their version of earthly paradise, their consolations of youth, the places for him and Nancy to capture rapture would eventually all change. And what would become of Le Clos? He and Nancy could live there together for a while, but in the end his brother's children would have to decide what to do with it.

~

The man who was always late, a little distracted, who regarded life as "essentially tragic", but embraced art, people, love and beauty was not concentrating on the practicalities in front of him. As always, there were too many thoughts of too many things pouring through his mind. In the same way that Nancy remembered him being late for their first train journey together, with exploding suitcases, lost items and his extraordinary ability to magnify happiness, nothing about him had essentially changed. Humphrey was the same, even in late middle-age. He was late. Again. He drove eight miles to the garage in Great Easton, collected the spare set of keys and jumped back into his car. He swung out onto the road and turned confidently to the right-hand side. Perhaps if they hadn't just returned from France he wouldn't have made the mistake. Perhaps if he hadn't been having a particular thought at that particular time he would have had a clearer mind. But he was not in France, he was in England. He was on the wrong side of the road and drove straight into the path of an oncoming lorry.

~

He had left Hill Pasture and Nancy for the last time.

CHAPTER THIRTY

Beyond the End

After 1971

It was Ernest's son, Julian Tennant, who broke the news to his aunt. Nancy retreated for several months to her sister Margaret's house. "I owe a special debt to my great nephews and nieces, for it is they more than anyone else, who put fun and purpose back into my life when, after Humphrey's death, all seemed lost," she declared years later at her 90th birthday party. She always claimed that Humphrey was '*the cat that walked alone*' but ultimately, she walked in tandem with him, creating their own version of partnership, loving friendship and rapturous happiness. She wrote later in life that her early realisation that she couldn't possess him gave him the freedom he needed. Without that freedom, yet without each other, the gardens may never have existed and continue to be "loved and cherished".

~

Hill Pasture's garden still survives but as an overgrown, wild version of its former self. The Goldfinger house features a large new extension and has become a family home. Although much of the garden has reverted to grass, some of the trees and shrubs that Humphrey and

Nancy's planting from the 1930's still grows with vigour. Chatsworth, although diminished, still travels determinedly uphill, drawing the eye to the top of the garden. The swimming pool trellis, today devoid of climbing roses and honeysuckle still frames the space, inviting a lingering gaze to the valley beyond. The part of the garden with the moongate is part of the neighbouring Ashgrove garden. The brickwork looks remarkably fresh, but now ivy sprawls over one side. What was the peaceful field in 1934 is no longer a slice of quiet English countryside. Hill Pasture lies under the flightpath of Stanstead Airport, which is a few minutes' drive away.

~

Nancy loved her great nieces and nephews and took a keen interest in all her relations. She was Godmother to Humphrey's nephew William. She considered Humphrey's family her family as they too, in turn regarded her as part of theirs. They all called her 'Aunt Nan'. It wasn't the blueprint of the 1950's cliché of a post-war woman finding satisfaction in domestic bliss. She had her own version of bliss and it wasn't the now largely abandoned myth. A woman's woman she was also a man's "heart". On 20th June, 1987 Nancy celebrated her 90th birthday surrounded by friends and Tennant and Waterfield relations. She made a speech. After thanking her sister Margaret, who was also still alive, as her "unfailing support", she turned to her younger relations, and said, *'you are growing up into a push-button world, a lot of your thinking will be done for you. Don't let this dull your sense of wonder. Think about the swallow who goes off to Africa for the winter and then comes back to its old nest . . . think about the snowdrop, when the first frost comes, you can try as hard as you like to get your fork into the ground, you won't succeed but up it comes all wibbly-wobbly with apparently no trouble at all. These are the things that matter.'*

~

Aged 104 she was guest of honour at the Bach Choir's 125th anniversary at the Royal Gala Performance in the Royal Opera House in recognition of her contribution to British choral music, with the Prince of Wales in attendance. On 24th July 2001 she wrote to her Tennant cousin, Tanera Averdieck, about the experience: *One special treat was the Centenary Concert of the Bach Choir on the 3rd of June. It took place in Covent Garden and because I'm the oldest member of the choir I was given three tickets, so Jay and Maggie were able to take me. I was a bit dubious about going but it was a lovely glamorous occasion. I got a little clap all to myself.'*

~

She often compared her relationship with Humphrey to a 'basket of eggs' with an unreliable handle, which threatened to fall off, but never did. Arguably she was considerably happier than countless women who did what was expected of them, or compromised for the sake of conventional romantic expectation. The strong little girl in the painting became the same determined woman who found romantic bliss as she felt she had with Humphrey. Humphrey re-ignited her youthful *joie de vivre* and she gave Humphrey the love and kindness he deserved. After their first holiday together she wrote, '*I have known complete happiness. I possess something which death and perhaps even that cannot take away.'*

She died peacefully in Essex on 13th March 2006 and was buried with Humphrey's easel.

Epilogue

Nancy never returned to Le Clos after Humphrey's death but the garden, tended by her Godson William Waterfield, and since his death in January 2021, his widow Judith Pillsbury, is still in essence Humphrey's creation. The garden remains a small vision of Eden. The magnificent wisteria continues to grow flamboyantly over the front of the villa. Palm leaves still catch the breeze. The *scala nobile* still invites a visitor (and there are still many) to enjoy the calm of dappled light on water, drawing the eye to the steady blue horizon of the Mediterranean Sea. There is a plaque on the garden wall in memory of Mario.

Venture into the cool of the villa and Humphrey's paintings still hang on the walls. There is one painting quite unlike his other landscapes and still life works. It is a semi-erotic composition of a group of young men sunbathing with a young woman in what appears to be a Riviera scene. An athletic, toned man is pulling off his top, revealing a perfect torso. Another sits tantalisingly close to him, his face almost brushing the front of his trunks. It is strikingly similar to Duncan Grant's 1920 painting, *Bathers by the Pond*, now hanging in Pallant House in Chichester. Grant's bathing scene is set at the pond at Charleston Farmhouse and is widely recognised as a homo-erotic fantasy. Whether Humphrey chose to copy it, prior to entertaining Vanessa Bell and Duncan Grant at Le Clos with Clive Bell is a possibility, transposing his version of Grant's painting into a Menton landscape as an exercise. Or did Grant begin the painting for Humphrey to complete? Is the group of beautiful, blank faced young men luxuriating on a jetty by a bright blue sea an expression of Humphrey's dream of a perfect youthful summer's day? Are they him, Peter and Hammy? Is the girl Nancy? Who knows. But turn away from what appears to be a homage to the famously magnetic Grant and a window onto Humphrey's sexuality and a very different painting catches the eye. An elegant older woman is concentrating on her task in hand. Her thick, grey hair is swept off her pale, handsome face. Her earrings catch the light. She sits at a table chopping vegetables with a large, white ceramic cooking pot beside her. It is a picture of peace. A contented smile dances across her face.

Of course it would. Humphrey loved Nancy and she loved him. Together they created their own version of earthly paradise with passion and no care for earthly convention, romantic expectation or social limitation. Hill Pasture might have appeared to be a solution to an unsatisfactory romantic misunderstanding in 1936, but it was exactly the opposite. Hill Pasture was the beginning of their life together. They were each other's greatest loves and they didn't want anything or anyone else. And in England and in France, the legacy of that love is still growing.

Hill Pasture, Broxted
Ashgrove Cottage, Broxted
Greys Court, Henley National Trust
Abbots Ripton Hall, Cambridgeshire
Le Clos Menton, France
The Chace, Ugley

Acknowledgements

The first person I must thank is the late William Waterfield, Humphrey's nephew and Godson to Nancy, who welcomed me to Le Clos in 2019. He gave me a detailed tour of the garden and showed me Humphrey's diaries and paintings. A gifted and well-known plantsman himself, as Humphrey's closest surviving relation, his recollections and perspective on his uncle were invaluable. His wife, Judith Pillsbury has been consistently enthusiastic and generous with her time and knowledge, without her help, many of Humphrey's letters, diaries and creations would have been forgotten and the story could not have been told as intimately. She is now that particular Eden's keeper, ensuring Le Clos du Peyronnet remains a vision of paradise and crucially, is protected as a French monument.

Tennant family help has come thick and fast from all directions, first, second and third cousins of Nancy have swung into action, searching through attic boxes for photographs, contacting old acquaintances on my behalf, humouring me with answering yet another question, looking through letters and dredging their memories of life decades ago. Without them, I could not have formed such a full-bodied impression of the characters in Eden's Keepers. I particularly want to thank Nancy's great nieces, Angie Tennant and her sister Nell Carey. Angie's energy and generosity of spirit buoyed my determination to begin the book in the first place. The painting of Nancy as a young girl and the drawing of Bunny Tennant hanging in Nell's house began the research process, along with Nell's other Tennant paintings, portraits, drawings and photographs. Without their help, such an intimate understanding of the family could not have been gained.

Other Tennant relations who have been of immense help include Tom and Finella Tennant who introduced me to William Waterfield and gave insight into life in Menton. Tanera, Edward and William Averdieck who variously found, sorted and shared photographs, letters and memories. Thank you too, to John Tennant, who not only shared invaluable memories of Ernest Tennant, but also fleshed out my understanding of Tennant and Gairdner family history and education. I must also thank Margaret Birley, who along with her siblings, have not only given me permission to quote from Nancy Tennant's unpublished memoirs, but supplied memories, photographs and fond recollections.

Thanks too to the staff at the Paul Mellon Centre and to Charlotte Brunskill in particular. It was a joy to sit in the beautiful Reading Room, researching month after month, year after year (with more than one lockdown hiatus), feeling each time I opened an archive box, I was staring into a treasure-trove of material. Other thanks go to Camilla and Tim Gardner, for sourcing and enlightening me on Gardner family history. Lynne Isham for welcoming Angie and me to Hill Pasture unannounced one sunny day and generously giving me insight into the garden, house and its architectural significance. Thank you to Camilla MacDonnell who gave me a window on and understanding of things Austrian and German and to Christopher Wentworth Stanley, for his encyclopaedic knowledge of all things Viennese and beyond. To Pip Morrison and Kim Wilkie for patiently giving me a crash course in the history of landscape gardening one evening, and whose garden is a vision of English Eden. Thanks to Edward Wake, for sharing his garden books, insight and sentimentality for lost gardens of childhood. To Alastair Barclay for his recollections of prep school life. Thank you also to Hugo Brunner for his insight on Humphrey and the garden at Greys Court. Thanks to Kirstie

Acknowledgements

Ritchie for helping me find Lady Salt and her daughter Charlotte Trower who shared their memories of Ugley village life. Thanks also to Charles Spicer, for sharing his knowledge and perspective on the Anglo-German Fellowship and Hamish McLean for introducing us. Further thanks to the following for their advice and encouragement. Dr Jean Cornell, Charlotte Eagar, Louisa Symington, Katie Fulford, Tiddy Maitland-Titterton, Giles Kime, Lisabel Miles, Humphrey Barclay, Alex Abberton, Miranda Averdieck, Clare Clark, Lucy Baring, Camilla Bashaarat, Becky Bagnell and Flora McLean and everyone at Clearview Books.

Thank you to my beloved Dingus, Alexander and Eliza who have lived with my obsession with this story for quite some time, pre, during and post lock-downs, listening to extracts, reading sections and always telling me it was interesting. Without the beauty of our own earthly paradise, I wouldn't have had the inspiration to write it.

Finally thank you to Patricia Barclay, without whom I would never have had a Cousin Nancy in my life at all.

Sarah Barclay, June 2022

Bibliography

The Long Afternoon Giles Waterfield, Headline Review 2001

Tennant's Stalk Nancy Crathorne, Macmillan 1973

Beyond Jerusalem Music in the Women's Institute 1919-1969 Lorna Gibson, Routledge 2008

Ribbentrop Michael Bloch, Transworld 1994

Broken Blood The Rise and Fall of the Tennant Family Simon Blow, Faber & Faber 1987

Jam Busters Julie Summers, Simon & Schuster 2014

Village Voices Piers Dudgeon, WI Books 1989

Waterfield's School Simon Wright, Herons Ghyll Press 1994

Henry 'Chips' Channon Edited by Simon Heffer, Hutchinson 2021

Women of the Raj Margaret Macmillan, Thames & Hudson 1988

Travellers In The Third Reich Julia Boyd, Elliot and Thompson Ltd 2018

The Glamour Boys Chris Bryant, Bloomsbury 2020

Appeasing Hitler Tim Bouverie, Vintage 2019

True Account Ernest W D Tennant, Max Parrish 1957

'Guilty Women', Foreign Policy, And Appeasement in Inter-War Britain Palgrave Macmillan 2015

The Fishing Fleet: Husband Hunting In The Raj Ann de Courcy, 2013 Weidenfeld & Nicholson 2013

Lanning Roper And His Gardens Jane Brown, Weidenfeld & Nicholson

UNPUBLISHED ACCOUNTS:
Some Recollections A D Gardner unpublished
Memoirs of A D Tennant unpublished

ARCHIVE SOURCES
The Paul Mellon Centre
Kings College Cambridge
University College Oxford
Library of the Society of Friends
The Women's Library London School of Economics
Country Life
House & Garden
Gardens Illustrated
Royal Horticultural Society
Imperial War Museum
Tennant and Gairdner private unpublished family letters and memoirs.

Index

Index